*Escape
from
Auschwitz*

Escape from Auschwitz

Erich Kulka

Foreword by Herman Wouk
Introduction by Yehuda Bauer

Bergin & Garvey
Westport, Connecticut • London

Library of Congress Cataloging in Publication Data

Kulka, Erich.
Escape from Auschwitz.
1. Auschwitz (Poland : Concentration camp)
2. Holocaust, Jewish (1939–1945)   3. Escapes—Poland.
4. Lederer, Siegfried.   I. Title.
D805.P7K77   1986   940.54′72′43094384   85–22825
ISBN 0–89789–088–4
ISBN 0–89789–089–2 (Pbk.)

British Library Cataloguing in Publication Data is available.

Copyright © 1986 by Bergin & Garvey Publishers, Inc.

All rights reserved. No portion of this book may be reproduced by any process or technique, without the express written consent of the publisher.

Library of Congress Catalog Card Number: 85–22825
ISBN: 0–89789–088–4
    0–89789–089–2 (pbk.)

First published in 1986

Bergin & Garvey, 88 Post Road West, Westport, CT 06881
An imprint of Greenwood Publishing Group, Inc.

Printed in the United States of America

The paper used in this book complies with the Permanent Paper Standard issued by the National Information Standards Organization (Z39.48–1984).

10 9 8 7 6 5 4 3 2

In remembrance
of my late wife

ELLY

who after surviving Theresienstadt and Auschwitz,
perished January 1945 in the
Nazi concentration camp Stutthof.

Contents

Foreword by Herman Wouk		ix
Preface		xi
Introduction by Yehuda Bauer		xiii
1.	The Manhunt Begins	1
2.	Theresienstadt Ghetto	3
3.	The Mass Grave	7
4.	The Transport	13
5.	On the Platform	19
6.	The Camp	25
7.	René	33
8.	You Have Nothing to Lose	39
9.	Operation "Heydebreck"	43
10.	Defend Yourselves	51
11.	Twelve Minutes, Eight Seconds!	59
12.	We Shall Escape in Uniforms	67
13.	The Password: Tintenfass	79
14.	In Plzen	89
15.	A Hiding Place	95
16.	The Weekend House at Zbraslav	101
17.	The Dealer in Documents	107
18.	Secretly in the Ghetto	113
19.	Message to Switzerland	119
20.	The Auschwitz Railway Station	127
21.	To the Partisans in Slovakia	135
Postscript		145
Appendix: About the Author		147

Photographs follow pages 32 and 94.

Foreword

THE AUTHOR OF *Escape from Auschwitz*, Mr. Erich Kulka, is a survivor of Auschwitz who became a serious historian of the Nazi era. We have many survivor accounts and diaries of European Jewry's vast tragedy; and we have numerous academic histories of the catastrophe, written by scholars who were not there. Mr. Kulka was there, and his scholarly works have a rare authoritative ring of personal testimony. In writing my novels of the Hitler period, *The Winds of War* and *War and Remembrance*, I consulted Mr. Kulka and his books for accuracy, and for authenticating detail.

In *Escape from Auschwitz*, Mr. Kulka has employed the fiction form to recount a true story which does not lend itself to the methods of academic history, but which sheds much light on the still enigmatic horror of the German massacre of the Jews. Mr. Kulka is not essaying the darkly poetic pictures of an Elie Wiesel, or the lighthearted suspense of a thriller writer. His aim remains historical accuracy and reality. However, to narrate this escape adventure, the records and the people having largely perished or vanished, he has used creative imagination to bridge the gaps, without departing from his central lifelong purpose: to bear true witness.

HERMAN WOUK

Preface

ESCAPES FROM THE HELL of Auschwitz were tried a hundred times, and a hundred times death was the reward for courage and protest. In their determination to escape from the constant threat of death, some Jewish prisoners were also seduced by attractive offers from corrupt SS members. Such escape plans led only to rewards for the treacherous SS, and torture and death for all prisoners involved.

This story is a historical account of the only known escape in which all Jews involved survived (the SS accomplice perished). I experienced some of these events personally, and verified the rest by questioning some of the survivors who I knew in the camps and who played major roles. All persons in the story really exist and most of the names used are genuine. I appear in the story under the name Karel Krasa.*

Three months after the German occupation of my native Czechoslovakia, in March 1939, I was arrested by the Gestapo for resistance activities. In 1940 I was deported from a prison in Brno to the concentration camp in Dachau; in 1941 I was sent to Neuengamme; and in the beginning of November 1942 I was sent to the extermination camps of Auschwitz-Birkenau, where I was tattooed with the number 73043. There I succeeded in acquiring a life-saving job in the prisoners' maintenance squad as locksmith and plumber. Thanks to this assignment, I could move relatively freely throughout most of the Auschwitz-Birkenau complex. Under the pretext of urgent repairs, I also gained access to the privileged Czech Family Camp, to which my first wife, Elly, and our ten-year-old son were deported from the

---

*This work is historically accurate. I have fictionalized only some materials based on my recollections and those of others.

Theresienstadt ghetto in September 1943. My relationship to them had to be kept secret from the SS, otherwise my access would be prohibited and I feared severe punishment. Thanks to my occupation, I became one of the few prisoners to maintain contact with the underground resistance movement in this strictly isolated family camp, where the hero of this story, the prisoner Siegfried Lederer, lived, and from which he escaped.

At that time I did not know the detailed story of Lederer's escape with his SS companion. I learned about it only twenty years later, during a chance meeting in Prague with Lederer, whom I knew from the camp. His story seemed too fantastic. Lederer, sensing my doubts, provided factual proof of his incredible adventure.

During the next two years I visited places connected with the story and interviewed people who had provided both escapees with refuge and help. Since survivors from both the Theresienstadt ghetto and Birkenau's Czech Family Camp certified most parts of Lederer's story, I decided to record in the form of a historical novel this unique attempt to warn the world and save the lives of the doomed.

In 1966 *Útek z tábora smrti* (An Escape from the Death Camp) was published in Prague. Two years later, the day the Russians invaded and occupied Czechoslovakia, I escaped from Prague and settled with my family in Israel. There I was able to contact Josef Neumann, an Auschwitz survivor closely involved in the events related here. Thus I can now present the complete story of this courageous and tragic escape, unique in the history of the Holocaust.

ERICH KULKA
Jerusalem

Introduction

VERY FEW PEOPLE escaped from Auschwitz. Even fewer survived to tell the story. The hundreds of books, the many thousands of testimonies, the many films that were made, cannot transmit even a faint idea of the reality of the Holocaust. But, for the sake of a hope that humankind will see the Holocaust as a warning, one has to continue trying to tell the story.

Erich Kulka's story has a context—a very complicated and involved one. The Nazi Party came to power in 1933 against the background of a terrible economic crisis, in the wake of the defeat of Imperial Germany in World War I, in the midst of a German population that began despairing of the possibility of a democratic solution to seemingly insoluble problems. Yet the Nazis came to power not by popular vote, but by an intrigue triggered by the fact that there was no working majority in the German parliament. In fact, in the last free elections of the German democratic "Weimar" republic, in November 1932, they lost two million votes and thirty-four parliamentary seats. Precisely because right-wing politicians thought that the Nazis were no longer a danger, they called them to power, believing that if only Hitler and two other Nazis were part of a conservative government, all the other members of which were non-Nazi right-wingers, they could rule Germany. Hitler, once in power, quickly brushed aside his erstwhile allies, and instituted a brutal dictatorship.

The Nazis did not come to power as a result of antisemitic propaganda. People who supported them did so overwhelmingly because of the combined issues of economics and nationalism, though everyone who voted for the Nazis knew the vote was for an antisemitic party. Though the Nazis did not make antisemitism their central plank, this was a purely tactical consideration. The inner core of the "true believers" saw the Jewish issue as central. They believed in a reordering of the European continent, and then of the world, in line with their racialist doctrines. Nordic peoples of the Aryan race—with the Germans as the purest Nordics leading the way—would rule the world, reorganize subject peoples such as the Slavs, and eliminate all possibility of a rebellion by mass murdering all potential opponents. The achievement of that goal was dependent, however, on the elimination of the Jews. In Nazi ideology the Jews were a satanic force, and at the same time a disease, a corrupting agent in the body politic of the nations of the world—an image that can be traced to traditional Christian antisemitic stereotypes depicting the Jews as possessed by the devil. In Nazi eyes, the Jews were trying to deny the Germans their proper role as the leaders of the nation. The idea of an international Jewish conspiracy, which today is presented to us by Soviet antisemitic propaganda, was a central tenet of faith for the Nazis. The Nazis believed that only war could solve basic human problems, and war was to be brutal and uncompromising. Their war would be directed, on the one hand, to assure the German people and their Nordic allies their proper "living space," and on the other hand it would be a titanic struggle against the Jewish world conspiracy. Even during the war, when it became so obvious that far from there being any Jewish conspiracy, the tiny Jewish minority in Germany and the Allied nations was not capable of saving even a remnant of Jews from the Nazi hell, and was incapable of uniting in an effort to plead for rescue, the Nazis persisted in their quasi-religious, fanatic belief.

Inherent in this ideology was murder. But neither Hitler nor any other Nazi chieftain spelled out, prior to 1939, what was to be done with and to the Jews. It seemed that though Jews were to be deprived of their rights, fired from their jobs, robbed of their property, tortured and humiliated, they would only be evicted from Germany—nobody planned mass murder. In early 1939, Hitler for the first time publicly stated that if another war broke out, the "Jewish race" in Europe would be annihilated. This was understood to be the vainglorious statement of a fanatic politician, not the outcome of a state decision. Indeed, there is absolutely no evidence of any planning for murder in 1939, or even in 1940. Murder was to become conscious to the perpetrators only in 1941, as the preparations for the invasion of the USSR were made, and millions of Jews, in addition to other European Jews, were to fall into Nazi hands. Previous plans to deport the Jews from Europe were dropped and, apparently, the decision was taken first to murder the Jews of the USSR by machine-gunning, and then, immediately afterwards, the "Final Solution" was extended to wherever the Germans could lay their hands on Jews. Special installations were built, beginning in 1941, to kill the Jews, who were to be misled and kept in the dark of their fate right until the last moment, so as to avoid any resistance or possible outside intervention.

Auschwitz was established in 1940 as a concentration camp for Polish political prisoners and, later, for Soviet prisoners of war. In the summer of 1941, at the behest of Heinrich Himmler, Auschwitz was designated by its commander, Rudolf Hess, as a future central murder installation for Jews. A first, experimental gassing with Zyklon B, a derivative of prussic acid gas, took place in Auschwitz on September 3, 1941. These first victims were largely Soviet POWs. Immediately afterwards, in October, preparations were made for what turned out to be the first operative killing center at Chelmno in western Poland, where masses of Jewish victims were killed in gas vans that transported them to woods where their bodies were interred or burned. Chelmno began operating on December 8, 1941. In March 1942 another killing center, at Belzec in southeastern Poland, began murdering the Jews of that region, and during the spring and early summer of 1942 the two death camps of Sobibor and Treblinka began to murder Jews. Belzec, Sobibor, and Treblinka were under one command, namely, that of the Lublin SS Commander, Odilo Globocnik. By that time Auschwitz became fully operative. By early 1943 it became the main killing center.

Jews were transported to the death camp from all over Nazi Europe. In the East, the Nazis had crowded the Jewish minorities into so-called ghettos (the original, late medieval ghetto had been a largely voluntary concentration of Jews in separate quarters for self-protection and community life). Starvation and disease were rampant there and demanded hundreds of thousands of victims. In the West, where no ghettos were established, Jews were collected and brought to the killing centers by train. They were told that in the East they would be able to earn their living by working under German supervision.

Most European Jews were killed from 1941 to 1943, without, in most cases realizing what their fate would be until they were already in the gas chambers. In the East, the local populations were largely indifferent to their fate, with a large minority being actively hostile, and a small, sometimes very small, minority actively friendly and helpful. Escape from camps was almost impossible, and even when it was successful, the problem was how to survive in the face of overwhelming hostility or indifference from the surrounding population.

By 1944, the only large Jewish populations still remaining in Europe were those of the Balkans, largely in Hungary and Rumania. Disaster was averted from the core of Rumanian Jewry in late 1942 because of a change of mind of the pro-Nazi local regime of strongman Ion Antonescu. In Hungary, on the other hand, the occupation of the country in March 1944 by the Nazis was disastrous. Adolf Eichmann, the SS officer chiefly responsible for the deportation of Jews to the death camps, managed to implement the concentration, humiliation, expropriation, marking, ghettoization, and deportation of Hungarian Jews to Auschwitz with lightning speed. This could only be done because of the full and enthusiastic cooperation of the Hungarian authorities, with the active or passive help of large segments of the Hungarian population. Between mid-May and early July of 1944, some 437,000 Jews were deported to Auschwitz, where most of them were gassed to death immediately upon arrival. Parallel with the Hungarian tragedy, transports arrived from other areas as well, including Theresienstadt (Terezin), a ghetto in Bohemia where the Nazis had concentrated the Jews of Bohemia and Moravia (the western part of Czechoslovakia), as well as older people, well-known west European Jewish figures, and Jewish German war veterans. These people were supposed to end their life in the "model" ghetto of Terezin, but in fact Terezin was a place where people died of starvation and disease, and from which many thousands were sent to their deaths in Auschwitz. Two such groups were held separately in Auschwitz for a period of six months, during which time they were treated differently from the other inmates—they were not killed, their children received some schooling by teachers among the people in the transport, they were not forced to do slave labor, and were generally treated in a way unheard of at Auschwitz. After six months each transport was sent to be gassed. The purpose of the Nazis in this is not clear to this day, though quite possibly they intended to bring foreign journalists or Red Cross people to Auschwitz and were looking for a group to be paraded before such visitors.

At Chelmno, gassings ceased in March 1943, but resumed again in early 1944. The camp was liquidated in January 1945. Belzec was liberated in 1943, as was Sobibor, in the wake of a successful revolt of the Jewish inmates. Treblinka, where another successful revolt broke out, continued operations for a short while thereafter. The gas chambers at Auschwitz were blown up and installations dismantled in November 1944. Close to six million Jews had perished. The Nazi aim to annihilate the whole of the Jewish people had been partly achieved. That is the general background to the story told in this book.

The story that Erich Kulka tells is not fiction. It is the true story of one of the more amazing escape episodes—every escape from Auschwitz was amazing—and it has implications for us that the perceptive reader will discern as he goes along. Among other things it shows how alone the people were who braved fates that were worse than the death that was the normal end in that abnormal hell; how difficult survival was even when Auschwitz was left far behind; how, indeed, in Nazi Europe Auschwitz was ever-present, especially to the Jew, who was part of the one group all of whose members had been sentenced to death for the one unforgivable and irreversible crime of having been born.

We have the choice between the Holocaust as a warning and the Holocaust as a precedent. Kulka's book is another stone in the mosaic that may help us to make up our minds.

YEHUDA BAUER

Escape from Auschwitz

Chapter 1

The Manhunt Begins

AT DAWN one chilly, foggy April morning, the prisoner barracks commanders, armed with sticks, chased the prisoners out for the morning roll call. The area between barracks quickly filled up with prisoners in striped jackets. Their shaved heads stood out against the fog. In the midst of the SS officers' sharp commands, the shouting Kapos, and barking dogs, a roaring noise of alarm sirens suddenly broke out. This time, however, they were not warning against an air strike.

A prisoner had escaped! The screaming sirens were to scare anybody in the vicinity who might think of giving shelter to the escapee. Telephones in the commander's office started ringing one after another. The commander of the Auschwitz Gestapo was busy sending a telegram message of warning:

JEWISH PRISONER IN PROTECTIVE CUSTODY LEDERER SIEGFRIED BORN 6.3.1904 IN ALBER DISTRICT TACHOV ESCAPED AT NIGHT 5 APRIL 1944 FROM THE CONCENTRATION CAMP AUSCHWITZ II STOP ALL INVESTIGATIONS SO FAR UNSUCCESSFUL STOP START SEARCHING INDEPENDENTLY STOP THE SS REICHSFUEHRER ALREADY INFORMED . . .

The manhunt had begun in Auschwitz and all over the Third Reich. Could he possibly escape? Was there any chance for a starved prisoner in a striped jacket to escape from a camp encircled by a double fence of barbed wire charged with high voltage? Even if the prisoner knew how to get through the chain of patrols, how would he fool the dogs? And who in the hinterland would dare shelter a marked man with a tattooed number on his arm when the penalty was death?

Did anyone try to escape from the reign of death that was Auschwitz, from where there was no escape? Yes, there were several hundred who tried. The successful ones, however, can be counted on the fingers of one hand. Siegfried Lederer was one of them. He also had a companion. This, however, the commander of the camp did not know.

The story of Siegfried Lederer started long before the roaring sirens of Birkenau's main watchtower. It started early one morning, as the embers of the ruins of a little village near Kladno were dying out.

Chapter 2

Theresienstadt Ghetto

ON MARCH 15, 1939, Hitler's armies invaded Bohemia and Moravia, and the Czechoslovak Republic was erased from the map of Europe. The occupied territories became a part of the Third Reich under the status *Protectorate Boehmen und Maehren.* By the implementation of the Nuremberg racial laws, Czechoslovak citizens of Jewish origin were deprived of their civil and human rights. Except for the Jewish community of Prague—which became the executive body of the *Zentrale fuer die Auswanderung der Juden* (Center for the Emigration of Jews)—all Jewish communities were banned. The main function of the Prague Jewish community was to register the Jews for "emigration," which really meant deportation.

In October 1941 a consultation of Nazi representatives with the Reichsprotektor, SS General Heydrich, took place at the Prague Castle. There it was decided that the city of Theresienstadt and its fortress would be transformed into a ghetto where all the Jews from Bohemia and Moravia would be concentrated before being sent to extermination camps. The representatives of the Jewish community of Prague were ordered to elaborate an outline for "self-government" in the

Theresienstadt ghetto, headed by the *Judenaeltestenrat*, whose chairman was Jakub Edelstein. The Jewish representative, unaware of the real intentions of the Nazis, welcomed the idea of the ghetto and cooperated in its realization. They believed that in the ghetto the Jews would have a chance to survive the war without being driven away from their native country. Their optimism was further strengthened by the Nazi-inspired rumors that the ghetto would actually be a way station for eventual transport to Palestine.

From November 1941 transports started to arrive at Theresienstadt—first from Prague, later from other centers located in larger cities of Bohemia and Moravia. At the concentration centers, Jews had to hand over their personal property and the keys from their apartments to the Nazi administration.

The fortress of Theresienstadt was founded in 1780 by Austrian Emperor Joseph II, near the juncture of the rivers Ohre and Elbe, some 60 kilometers north of Prague. Before its transformation into a ghetto, the city of Theresienstadt had 3,500 inhabitants and the fortress served as military barracks. Theresienstadt was composed of two parts: the Small Fortress and the Big Fortress. The Small Fortress had been transformed by the Gestapo into a prison for political detainees in 1940. From the Big Fortress the ghetto was created. The army units were relocated and the deported Jews were placed in the barracks. From the outside, the ghetto was guarded by Czech gendarmes and from the inside by the SS. A strict regime for the prisoners was enforced, violations of which were punished by severe beating. In January 1942 nine prisoners were publicly hanged in Theresienstadt for maintaining contact with the "Aryan" population and for smuggling letters out of the ghetto. The so-called Jewish self-government—the *Judenaeltestenrat*—was merely an instrumental body, carrying out orders of the commander, SS Obersturmfuehrer Siegfried Seidel. The prisoners worked at rebuilding the ghetto, in agriculture and in various workshops, working on orders of the German armament industry. The prisoners got very little food, but their situation improved when they were allowed to write letters and receive food parcels from friends and relatives outside. The prisoners gradually improved their living conditions. Three-tiered wooden bunks were installed to increase space, and some privacy was achieved by inserting partitions into the big barrack rooms. In each room, one of the prisoners was responsible for order and a prisoner was also appointed over each barrack building.

In the evenings, after work, prisoners would get together in the barrack basements for cultural activities: evenings of reading, poetry recitals, singing, and playing music. Any hopes of surviving the war in

Theresienstadt were shaken, however, upon the first deportations in spring 1942. The mysterious eastward-bound transports to an unknown destination caused anxiety among the prisoners, and everyone did his best to avoid being selected for them. The transports were ordered by the SS command, which instructed the representatives of the *Judenaeltestenrat* to select a certain number of prisoners for a specified date. In the first years, disabled, ill, and old prisoners were not selected for the transports. This practice was designed to support the credibility of the SS, who had reassured the *Judenaeltestenrat* that these were working transports. Nor were well-known writers, artists, scientists, industrialists, bankers, and other personalities placed on transport lists at the beginning. These people were given some other privileges as well, such as permission to send letters to friends, even those abroad. This was intended to enhance Nazi propaganda, which presented Theresienstadt as a privileged ghetto. Members of the *Ghettowache* (ghetto guard), *Judenaeltestenrat*, and their families were also exempted from deportations to the east.

The influx of Jews into Theresienstadt grew steadily, and by the end of spring 1942 there were 20,000 prisoners in the ghetto. Since the capacity of the military barracks was exhausted, the SS command ordered the evacuation of all non-Jewish residents from Theresienstadt. Some two hundred houses and all the public buildings were placed at the *Judenaeltestenrat*'s disposal. Working units of prisoners speedily prepared the evacuated flats for the arriving prisoners. Three-tiered wooden bunks were quickly built into the rooms and straw bags were placed in the attics; stone floors of basements and stables were covered with layers of straw.

Another category of prisoners started to arrive at Theresienstadt. Trains from Austria and Germany brought men and women who were around sixty years old. For the most part, they were rich and formerly influential Jews, some bringing with them high military decorations from the First World War. Before coming to Theresienstadt, they signed contracts for the purchase of a new house with the officials of the SS *Heimeinkaufsvertraege*. For huge sums of money, they bought from the SS fully furnished flats with guaranteed medical care for the rest of their lives in the prominent *Altersghetto*. After their arrival at Theresienstadt, however, when they demanded that the contracts be honored, they were robbed of their remaining personal property and ruthlessly pushed onto wooden bunks and straw sacks in the dusty attics, dirty houses, stables, and damp cellars. Most of them died there within a few weeks. The death toll grew rapidly. Mass funerals became a part of daily life, and behind the walls of the city, furnaces were being constructed.

Chapter 3

The Mass Grave

IT WAS DAWN. The June night was receding. The wind was scattering the clouds hanging over the town of Theresienstadt. The contours of the town fortification showed up in the moonlight. Above them, the silhouettes of gendarmes were gliding noiselessly. A three-ton Opel-Blitz truck passed through the gate of the Sudeten barracks and stopped in the square courtyard. Four SS officers with helmets and machine guns jumped out of the truck onto the uneven pavement of the yard. A man in a gray-green uniform emerged from the driver's cab. He was tall and well built. The silver thunderbolts on his sleeves and the small squares in the facings of his uniform revealed his rank: SS Scharfuehrer.

He stood in the middle of the ghetto barracks yard with a whip protruding from one of his gleaming black boots. With his right hand he opened the holster in which his pistol hung on his belt, with the left he lit a long torch. Beams of light lingered for a moment in the dark corners of the yard, then moved to the front of the two-story house. The blackout was complete; not a trace of light came from behind the windows. There was silence. The Scharfuehrer took a whistle from his breast pocket and sent forth a piercing sound into the darkness. After a while, the blackout of the staircase windows was framed by a narrow strip of light. A sturdy prisoner came running out the door; he was George Petschauer, a member of the *Ghettowache*. He stopped short, surprised at the sight of a stranger disturbing the stillness of the night. He saw the four armed men in uniform standing near the truck and noted the silver skull and bones on their lapels.

SS Scharfuehrer Kurt Plagge scrutinized the prisoner. Before Petschauer had time to realize that he ought to report, the SS officer cracked his whip and barked; *"Los! Hundert Saujuden zum Sonderappel sofort antreten!"* (A hundred Jewish pigs will line up immediately!)

The ghetto policeman ran back to the barracks. There, all hell broke loose. The guards began treading on the sleeping prisoners, whose straw sacks covered the narrow strips of floor. The prisoners, urged on by the guards, jumped from the wooden bunks, drowsy, half dressed, and confused. They rushed down the staircase to the yard. There they were blinded by the headlights of the truck. The guards of the *Ghettowache*, led by Petschauer, lined up the prisoners and counted out a hundred.

Scharfuehrer Plagge shouted, "Every third prisoner forward!"

He examined the thirty-three men who stepped forward and his eyes rested on one of them. The Scharfuehrer drew nearer and lit his face with the torch. He was met with a firm look from blue eyes set in a sharply angled face with a strong chin. He stuck the thick end of his whip into the prisoner's leather jacket.

"Report!" he hissed.

"Prisoner in protective custody Siegfried Lederer, transferred from the Small Fortress," replied the prisoner in perfect German. He stood erect, neither moving nor averting his eyes.

"Shoes and shirts to be left here!" the Scharfuehrer said. He snapped his whip at thirty-three half-naked prisoners, chasing them into the truck. Petschauer was the last to jump in. The prisoners sat down on the floor, the SS officers occupied the back of the truck, and the driver revved up the engine. The prisoners were jammed into a small space; in both corners near the driver's cab there were open barrels of lime chloride. There were also picks and shovels between them.

The prisoners had been so stunned by this unexpected night assault that they had done or said nothing. Only when the ghetto gates closed behind them did they realize what it all meant: they were leaving for an unknown world, full of danger and horror. From the newspapers smuggled into Theresienstadt and from the radio they secretly listened to, they knew that martial law had been imposed following the assassination of Reichsprotektor Heydrich. Why should the Nazi vengeance on the Czech people stop at the ghetto gates? The prisoners' worst fears were realized; there could be no doubt about it. Barrels full of lime chloride. Picks and shovels. The squad of executioners with skulls and bones. This was the end. They were being taken to their execution and would be forced to dig their own graves. Four machine guns were pointed at them to suppress any thoughts of resistance. The SS formed a gray-green wall, making it impossible for the prisoners to see the countryside they were passing through.

Young George Petschauer wanted to know where they were being taken. He was waiting for an opportunity to ask. One of the barrels shifted a little when the truck took a sharp turn. The picks leaning against the barrel fell over. Petschauer rose to stand them up again, but he was immediately knocked down by an officer's boot. "Whoever moves will be shot without further warning!" said the commander of the squad.

Siegfried Lederer's mind was working furiously. He looked at his comrades. Most of them were young and strong. Thirty-three against six. More than five to one. They were not bound and they had nothing to lose. It would not be difficult to attack the SS officers. If they all moved at once, the SS would not have time to shoot. The Scharfuehrer and his driver could also be overpowered. The prisoners could take over the truck. But what then? They would drive on and fight their way through! But Lederer knew that, in the end, there was no escape. Yet they would not go as sheep to the slaughter. They would fight. Lederer looked around, trying to read his comrades' faces. He searched for a spark of life. But there was only fear in their eyes.

Next to Lederer, close to the left side of the truck, sat a thin, unshaven old man named Rudolf Steiner. He was looking through a hole in the canvas, observing the countryside moving past them. The truck was just passing a signpost. "We are heading toward Kladno," Steiner whispered to his neighbor. Before there was time for the message to reach all the prisoners, the truck made a turn onto a dirt road. They reached a village. A *Schuppo* squad (German police) equipped with dogs and machine guns was waiting for the prisoners. The prisoners jumped down from the truck and unloaded the tools. They were marched by the SS across the village green to a little pond. What the prisoners saw was a shocking scene: smoke and flames were rising from the ruins of farmhouses all around. Rabbits, hens, goats, and sheep ran between the smoldering ruins of cottages. Frightened pigeons could be seen on the roofs. And in front of them, ducks and geese were floating on the pond stirring the quiet water.

Scharfuehrer Kurt Plagge stopped the marching men. He ordered the prisoners to stand around the edge of the pond. He forced Lederer, Petschauer, Steiner, and sturdy little Otto Popel to jump into the water. They were to drive the birds out of the pond into the hands of the prisoners who were standing ashore. The SS amused themselves by pushing those standing ashore into the pond. The prisoners were ordered to bring the captured birds to a nearby stable, close to a farmhouse. An SS officer with a terrifying Alsatian dog stood at the door. Scharfuehrer Plagge, pointing his pistol at the prisoners, was highly amused by the scene. He laughed and slapped his thigh whenever the dog lunged at one of the prisoners and tore off a piece of his trousers. The prisoners, exhausted and dripping wet, were then lined up and taken by the SS to a farmhouse. There, a dreadful sight awaited them. In the garden behind the barn under the fruit trees, in irregular rows, lay the bodies of men who had been shot to death. The prisoners' fears were confirmed. They stood motionless. They had never seen such a harvest of death. They could only assume that they, too, would be led to the bullet-ridden straw mattresses hanging on the farmhouse wall. Another squad of SS joined the *Schuppo* escort. They encircled the prisoners, their machine guns ready to fire.

"Prisoners in the first line, take three steps forward!" ordered Plagge, just like in Theresienstadt in the morning. The tension grew. The prisoners were waiting for the final blow. Lederer whispered to Petschauer, "When you hear the order, fall down to the ground." But the order did not come. The fingers on the triggers did not budge. Kurt Plagge walked several times through the lines of prisoners. He was enjoying himself. He relished his role as stage director in this sadistic game with death. He pointed to the rows of bodies and said in a threatening voice, "Whoever will not follow my orders will end up like them."

The men in the first line, led by Petschauer, were ordered to remove the dead men's shoes and search through their clothes. The second line, which included Lederer, was to mark a rectangle on the ground among the trees.

Two open command cars stopped on the road in front of the farmhouse. A group of civilians and officers in gray-green and black uniforms emerged. Some carried cameras. Scharfuehrer Plagge saluted the commander of the group, and the visitors dispersed among the houses. The cameras clicked and buzzed, recording Hitler's reprisal for the assassination of Nazi Reichsprotektor Heydrich in Prague. Some posed in grotesque heroic positions, their "enemy" at their feet.

Some of the visitors drew near the prisoners to see what was taken out of the pockets of the murdered men. They raked with pointed sticks the objects heaped up on the ground and speared them when they wanted to examine them more closely. Plagge admired a leather wallet. He threw away the photographs and letters and took out several bank notes. These he folded carefully, passed them on to the *Schuppo* commander, and instructed him, "Make a list of all cash, rings, and watches. The rest of the things put into bags."

The group of reporters and officers examined the place of execution from all angles. Scharfuehrer Plagge replied to their questions and gave explanations, pointing to the burning houses, the erupting geysers of stone and dust, the frightened sheep. One of the officers wanted to know the purpose of the rectangular space in the middle of the garden.

"That is the mass grave. We will bury them in their native soil. We are not barbarians."

It was nearly midday. The sun was very hot, but the prisoners from Theresienstadt dug without stopping to rest or take food or drink. The SS guards lit fires all around and roasted the ducks and geese on wooden spits. They chewed the drumsticks greedily, the fat dripping from their chins onto their uniforms. Wiping their greasy hands in newspapers, they threw the trash, the clean picked bones, at the prisoners.

Deathly tired, exhausted by heat, hunger, and thirst, old Steiner could hold his pick no longer: it fell out of his hands for the third time. Lederer's encouragements and assistance did not help anymore.

"I cannot go on," Steiner groaned and held his head in his hands, leaning in despair over the edge of the pit.

Scharfuehrer Plagge, walking around the working prisoners like a watchdog, observed every move.

"What's wrong?" he roared at Steiner. The old man neither moved nor answered. Plagge rushed at him and kicked him into the pit. He stood at the edge of the mass grave with his legs wide apart, a pistol in his hand, carefully watching Lederer, who worked with the pick furiously, so as to give the Scharfuehrer no reason to move against him. Plagge was waiting for his opportunity. His eyes wandered from Lederer to Steiner. His nostrils flared as if scenting the prey. But with Steiner lying motionless and Lederer working diligently, he put his pistol back in its holster and left.

Once the danger had passed Lederer could attend to his wounded friend. He looked for something with which to wipe the blood off Steiner's face. He saw a crumpled piece of paper at the bottom of the pit and he flattened it out on his knee. It was the first page of the Prague newspaper *Der Neue Tag*. His attention was drawn to an article printed in heavy type: " . . . the inhabitants of the village of Lidice have violated the law by assisting the assassins of SS Reichsprotektor

Heydrich. Therefore, all the village men were shot, the women taken into concentration camps, and the children taken to places where they will receive proper education. The houses were destroyed and the name of the village erased off the map."

Lederer understood. He quickly hid the paper in his trouser pocket. He tore a piece of cloth from his underwear and bandaged the wound on Steiner's head.

"I can't pull through. This is the end," groaned Steiner. "But my daughter must stay alive. You know whom to contact and where my foreign accounts are. Send a message to her through Holzer. She will help you . . ." He fainted in the middle of the sentence.

The prisoners of Theresienstadt worked till late at night. It was growing dark when Scharfuehrer Plagge gave the order to have some wooden beams from the ruined buildings brought to the edge of the pit. Petrol was poured over them, and in this frightful illumination the prisoners buried the men of Lidice. Lederer counted 172 bodies.

A stray dog came whining to the graveside when the bodies of two boys, about sixteen years old, were being placed in the grave. Plagge fired his pistol.

"The dog will be buried along with the other dogs," he said and kicked the animal's body into the pit.

In the early hours of the morning the worn-out prisoners were ready to be driven back to Theresienstadt. A group of SS officers stood near the truck. One of them, Hans Rhode, an inspector from the Prague Gestapo, leaned against the door of a black Mercedes smoking a cigar. He watched the prisoners laying the unconscious Steiner on the floor of the car. Lederer heard Rhode saying to Plagge, "All these men know too much; they must soon disappear in the east."

Chapter 4

The Transport

ONCE A WEEK, a barber named Vaclav Vesely would come to the Theresienstadt barracks from a nearby village called Travcice. On that day the guardroom became a barber shop. The small room adjacent to the guard station filled with smoke. The guards, some in uniforms, some in their civilian clothes, sat on a bench, waiting to be attended to. The barber was soaping, rinsing, slapping, wiping, and powdering the fat faces of the Czech *Ghettowache*. On a narrow bench, behind the backs of the guards, there was a big black leather briefcase full of cloths, napkins, and barber's tools. Lederer took the bibs out carefully, but left the napkins among which some letters were folded. Once in a while, when none of the guards were looking, he took the letters out, one by one, and hid them inside his jacket. Then he inconspicuously left the room. Miroslav Zeimer came in to replace him. After a while, Lederer returned, deftly put a pack of letters into a briefcase, took a clean napkin, shook it out, and tied it around the next guard's neck. Then he retired to the corner to prepare for the next customer. Pretending to clean the shaving brush, he unscrewed its hollow wooden handle and put a piece of paper into it. On the paper, there was only a name and address: "Josef Cernik, tailor, Plzen, Doubravka." He then carefully watched the barber. When the barber paused from his brush work, Lederer drew closer to him, handed him the clean brush, and whispered, "Tell the tailor to hurry up. We may be transported soon."

The transports came sooner than Lederer expected. At the beginning of September 1943, before the message reached the tailor, two eastbound transport trains left from Theresienstadt. Lederer and Zeimer were included in the deportation lists, but at the last moment Leo Holzer, commander of Theresienstadt's fire brigade, managed to obtain an exemption for them. Holzer, who was also a member of the *Judenaeltestenrat*, managed to convince the SS officials that Lederer and Zeimer were indispensable to the fire brigade. They were both taken off the train just before its departure.

There were heartbreaking scenes on the platform. Families were separated, old friends and lovers said good-bye.

After the transport left, Theresienstadt was quiet, as if after a tempest. For the next two days, the prisoners talked about nothing but the transport. They were sorry for those who left, but in two months time rumors about other transports leaked out. Lederer and Zeimer were summoned at the second transport in December, and this time no intervention could help them.

At the Bohusovice-Theresienstadt railway station, railway employees, guarded by the SS, readied the train for departure. The doors of the cars gave a last ruthless creak and the deportees were cut off from the civilized world. The workers secured the doors with hooked nails and twisted wire. Scharfuehrer Plagge went from one car to another, stamping a seal on each door. He stopped at the last car and took a black folder out of his briefcase. It was inscribed "DS Transport Theresienstadt 18.12.1943." He looked through the lists of names. He stopped his finger on some of them and then wrote distinctly next to Lederer's name "RU," for *Rueckkehr unerwuenscht* (return undesirable).

Inside the cars things were in a state of chaos. Some cried, others shouted. Orders were heard but nobody paid much attention. Some sat on their luggage, which lay on the floor; they were resigned, apathetic to all that was happening. Others hoped the transport might mean another chance. They tried not to despair and to sustain their hopes. They tried to organize things, divide the space, and decide whose turn it was to stand, sit, or sleep. They shifted the luggage to make a little more room and to make the small barred window accessible.

A black Mercedes approached the platform. Commissar Rhode was seated next to the driver. Plagge stood at attention, saluted with his right hand, and announced, "Herr Obersturmfuehrer, a special train with 2,503 Jewish prisoners is ready for departure." Commissar Rhode took the deportation papers. He went over each page, adding some notes here and there. Then he put these, together with a letter, into a big stiff envelope and sealed it. He looked up and glanced at the train. His eyes stopped for a moment at Lederer's composed face, which appeared in the window of the last car. Plagge took his whistle and gave the signal for departure. As the train started to move, Plagge jumped into one of the cars where the other SS officers were already sitting, their helmets on their heads.

Behind the small windows of the cars, which were crossed with barbed wire, faces were continually changing. Nervous and fluttering eyes peered through the peepholes from behind the barbed wire. They saw the changing kaleidoscope of fields, rivers, villages, towns, and railway stations and tried to guess where they were headed. Is it going to be better there than it was in Theresienstadt? Or worse still? Who knows?

At the same time, hundreds of deportation trains were crawling through Europe like giant snakes. They came from Russia, Poland, Czechoslovakia, Yugoslavia, Rumania, Bulgaria, Greece, Holland, Denmark, Norway, Austria, France, Italy, Belgium, and Germany. They all had the same destination: Auschwitz.

In each train car, about eighty people were squeezed together. After a few hours, the pungent smell of excrement, overflowing from a single small bucket, poisoned the air. The children cried, but their mothers had no strength to console them. Several old people died during the night. They were laid along the side of the car, one on top of the other, and covered with a blanket. In the last car were the members of the Theresienstadt fire brigade. Among them were Lederer and his friend Miroslav Zeimer. Rudolf Steiner, former executive clerk of a bank in Plzen, was also in the car. His thoughts were of his daughter, who was born of a mixed marriage. Gitta meant everything to him. She was only ten years old when her mother died. After the implementation of the Nuremberg Laws in occupied Bohemia, Steiner managed to obtain for Gitta new personal documents stating that she was of Aryan origin. He sent her away to his deceased wife's relatives who lived in the village of Stupno, near Plzen. Soon after that, the Nazi persecution of Steiner began. It was discovered by Eichmann's Emigration Office that Steiner had not declared all the money he had abroad, a crime punishable by death. Steiner, a representative of the Jewish community, was sent to Theresienstadt on the next transport. Before his departure, Gitta came to say good-bye to him. She was eighteen years old and very attached to her father.

Less than three months later he was surprised to see her in a forestry station near Theresienstadt. Without his knowledge, she had arranged for her father to be included in a group of prisoners who worked in the woods, outside the Theresienstadt ghetto. Gitta would come to the forestry station once a month on a prearranged date. She would bring him linen, food, cigarettes, and letters for his friends. Just before Christmas, Steiner's visits with his daughter stopped.

Now he sat in the railway car, head in hands. His only wish was to see his daughter one last time. What is she going to do? Will she ever hear from me, know that I had to leave? Who will keep the contact between us? Where am I being taken? If only I could send her a message. If only I could write.

In the inside pocket of his coat Steiner had an unfinished letter to his daughter. He sat down on one of the suitcases in the corner of the car and added a few lines to the letter. He wrote on the envelope, "Please, kindly send this letter to the following address." He then made his way to the small barred window and threw out the folded letter. According to his calculations, the train was still in Czech territory and there was a chance that Gitta would receive the letter. Maybe it would be found by someone willing to help. The sudden creak of the brakes interrupted his thoughts. Shouts and curses could be heard from outside. The heavy gate creaked open and the burly face of Scharfuehrer Plagge appeared.

"Who threw out a letter?"

There was silence.

"Well?" barked Plagge and looked with his hateful eyes from one face to the other. Freezing December air seeped into the car, but the prisoners did not feel the cold. They were too scared. They saw Plagge take out his pistol and heard the click of the trigger.

"I give you one minute to tell me who threw the letter out. If I hear no answer I'll shoot all of you!"

Old Steiner slowly got up from the suitcase. "I threw it out, but it was only a piece of paper."

"You know it is strictly forbidden!" From Scharfuehrer Plagge it sounded like a death sentence. Steiner grew pale. Plagge brandished his revolver. The others did not understand. They heard the shot and Steiner fell, bleeding. He was still breathing. Plagge drew closer and put the pistol to his left temple. He shot again and kicked the dead body over.

The sliding wooden gate closed with a bang and it was dark again inside the car. Lederer and Zeimer covered the body of their dead friend with a blanket. Nobody uttered a word. Death had become an everyday affair. It was everywhere. It was traveling with them in the train and everybody was within its reach.

The journey continued. People took turns at the window and told the others the names of the railway stations they were passing: Dresden . . . Rylowitz . . . Gleiwitz . . . Early the next morning, Lederer took his turn at the observation post. The train was just arriving at a station. Lederer read the badly lit signpost: "Auschwitz." This time the brakes creaked harder.

Lederer turned to Zeimer and said, "It seems our journey ends here."

Chapter 5

On the Platform

THE DOORS OF THE CARS banged open one after the other. A stench carried out of the cars into the frosty December morning. Endless rows of barbed wire covered with frost could be seen all around; they were illuminated by strings of electric bulbs fixed on concrete poles. Strange, grotesque figures with bowl-like caps on their clean-shaven heads, in striped prisoner's garb, rushed into the cars. One could make out only part of what they were yelling: *"Alle raus! Vsichni ven! Wystepowacz!"* (All out!) Everybody was driven out: men, women, children, the old, and the sick.

The space between the railway cars and the barbed wire fences was closed off by a row of armed guards. Every other one held by its leash a furious-looking Alsatian. Behind the guards one could see rows of canvas-roofed army trucks and Red Cross ambulances. The men in prison garb ran among the confused newcomers like sheep dogs. They tried to organize them and prevent utter confusion by pushing, gesticulating, and shouting: *"Zu fuenften antreten! Ustavte se do petic! Ustawicz po pieciu!"* (Line up in groups of five!). They also urged the newcomers to leave their luggage behind, assuring them that it would be delivered to them in the camp. They even took the women's handbags. SS officers holding heavy clubs in their hands and armed with pistols stood at the side smoking, carefully watching the rushing about and the work of the men in stripes. At first sight, the officers looked good-natured. They mixed with the deportees and tried to calm them down, reassuring the suspicious in order to avoid trouble or resistance.

While Lederer and Zeimer carried a body out of the truck, one of the uniformed prisoners took Lederer's luggage and leather briefcase. Lederer protested. There was a skirmish and Zeimer came to help his friend. The man in stripes, seeing he was up against two, gave up. Still holding onto the briefcase, he whispered to Lederer, "The briefcase won't save you. If you want to live, volunteer to work. If you are lucky, you will look like me tomorrow. The others will all go up in smoke." He looked in the direction of the large buildings in the background, where the rows of barbed wire seemed to meet. They could see the red tiled roofs, illuminated by flames coming out of low broad square chimneys. The man in stripes disappeared before Lederer had a chance to understand his words.

The uniformed prisoner's attention was drawn to an elegant little suitcase held by a pretty young woman who was supporting her ill mother. With her free hand she tried to hold on to her belongings. In the ensuing scuffle the lid of the suitcase opened and its contents fell out onto the dirty platform. Just then a khaki-colored car with a clearly visible Red Cross symbol came along the road next to the tracks. The sick old woman straightened up, her feverish eyes opened wide.

"Look, René," she said excitedly, grasping her daughter's hand firmly. "There is an ambulance! Surely, there will be a doctor there. Let's go and ask for help!"

The man in stripes, who was bending down and carefully collecting the rich contents of the suitcase, got up and whispered in a low voice, "The doctors in Auschwitz do not cure, and the Red Cross does not help. Don't say you are ill. There is no medicine inside the car, only gas, which will suffocate you in the gas chambers. This is your final stop and you will not need any of the things you have brought with you."

The ambulance stopped in the middle of the railway platform. A young officer got out. He had black eyes and a well-cut uniform. He advanced toward the groups of Theresienstadt prisoners. The young woman and her mother met him midway and the mother implored him in good German, "Sir, I am very ill and I beg you to help me. They want to poison us. Please, protect us!"

The officer saluted politely, offered some pills that would calm their nerves, and asked who told them such nonsense.

"That one, with the black suitcase," cried the sick lady and pointed to the man in stripes who was carrying their belongings to the heap of luggage.

"My dear ladies," said the officer in a friendly voice, "I promise you that nothing will happen to you. You should not believe these convicts. They try to frighten you in order to get hold of your luggage. I promise you, you will not be molested anymore."

The officer was the physician, SS Hauptsturmfuehrer Dr. Josef Mengele. He looked for somebody who would see to it that the two women would not spread a panic. He waved his hand, and out of the nearby group of SS, a tall young soldier quickly strode forth.

"Rottenfuehrer Viktor Pestek reporting."

"Take care of these two ladies, Rottenfuehrer," ordered Mengele. "Find out who took their suitcase and make sure that it is returned to them."

Pestek looked at the slender figure of the blue-eyed, fair-haired young woman standing there alone with her mother. He smiled and blew his whistle. A short fat prisoner with a red-and-yellow Star of David on his shirt rushed toward them. His red face and red-blue nose suggested he was a drinker. The ribbon on his sleeve had an inscription: *Kapo-Aufraeumungskommando* (clearing-up brigade). He was a prominent prisoner; the commander of a prisoner brigade called him "Canada."

Before he had time to report, Rottenfuehrer Pestek commanded, "See to it that these two ladies get to the camp safely and that their belongings are returned to them!"

Nobody paid any attention to Scharfuehrer Plagge, who stood on the side, looking at the bustle on the platform. When the Theresienstadt prisoners got into formation, Plagge went to a group of officers in leather coats who were standing near the ambulance. Plagge gave the "Heil Hitler" salute, presented his report, and handed a big envelope to the officer in charge, a man with high cheekbones and a sharp, pointed nose.

SS Untersturmfuehrer Johann Schwarzhuber opened the envelope, took the transport lists out, and without saying a word handed them to the man beside him, an SS officer from the political department. He then took a letter out of another carefully sealed envelope marked *Geheime Reischssache* (Strictly Confidential) and read, "To the commander of the concentration camp in Auschwitz: by order of the RSHA take over 2,503 Jewish prisoners from the Theresienstadt ghetto. They are to be held for a six-month quarantine. Families are to be placed in the same camp together with the prisoners of the Theresienstadt transports DL and DM that came on 7 September 1943. The date and the manner of special treatment will be decided by the head of department IVa 4b Adolf Eichmann of the Reich's security headquarters in Berlin. Signed: SS Hauptsturmfuehrer Hans Guenther, head of the Central Emigration Office in Prague."*

Schwarzhuber returned the letter to its envelope, turned to the officers, and said, "Gentlemen, I won't need you anymore; there will be no selection today."

He turned to the nearest ambulance, opened the driver's cab, and got in. Behind the little glass window could be seen a pile of gray-green tins with the inscription "Zyklon B." Schwarzhuber ordered the loudspeakers on. The driver put a key into the dashboard. The control light lit up and a barely audible hum could be heard. Schwarzhuber took the microphone off its hook and in a sweet, consoling voice announced, "You are now in a new settlement area of the working camp Birkenau, and under the protection of the SS. Keep calm! You will be subject to special hygienic and sanitary measures. You will live in a special family camp. Your luggage will be taken there. Soon postcards will be distributed and you will be able to write to your relatives and friends. No harm will be done to those who follow our instructions."

The ambulance turned toward the main guard building. SS physician Mengele reported to Schwarzhuber as he was getting out of the car. He mentioned the incident with the suitcase.

"Find out that prisoner's number," ordered Schwarzhuber. Then he disappeared into the guard commander's office.

About half an hour later, thirty men in prison uniforms, led by the Kapo of the clearing-up brigade, lined up in front of the guardhouse. On the other side stood the SS officers responsible for maintaining order on the platform. A wooden bench was placed between the two groups. Schwarzhuber came forward and the red-faced Kapo presented his report. When he finished, Schwarzhuber asked, "Were all the prisoners of the clearing-up brigade told before starting work that they are forbidden to speak to newcomers?"

"They were," assured the Kapo.

"Is there anyone who did not know?" asked Schwarzhuber, looking around.

There was silence.

Schwarzhuber continued, "Do any of you know about, or has any one of you seen or heard about, people from a transport being killed in a Birkenau gas chamber?"

---

* For a discussion of the Theresienstadt-Auschwitz connection, see E. Kulka, "Terezin A Mask for Auschwitz," in *Terezin 1941-1945,* published by the Council of Jewish Communities in the Czech Lands, Prague, 1965, pp. 182-203.

Nobody spoke. Schwarzhuber again broke the tense silence. "Listen to the verdict."

The guard commander read aloud, "It has been ascertained that prisoner number 36950, member of the clearing-up brigade, with the aim of agitating and creating panic among the prisoners who arrived from Theresienstadt, frightened women by telling them alarming tales about gas chambers. He is sentenced to one hundred strokes of the whip. The sentence will be carried out by the members of the clearing-up brigade. Every man five strokes. Whoever refuses to carry out the order will be punished by fifty strokes. The Kapo of the clearing-up brigade, who did not maintain the group's discipline, is demoted and sentenced to one year's labor in the penal brigade."

A Slovak prisoner, number 36950, was called. He stepped forward. "Trousers down," ordered Dr. Mengele. He quickly examined the prisoner. "Fit for the penalty," said Mengele and approved the sentence with his signature.

Two SS officers tied the prisoner to a wooden bench with leather thongs. The Kapo gave the first five strokes of the lash. The victim stopped counting after fifty strokes and fainted after seventy. The commander of the guards ordered the prisoners to go on till the last stroke. The near-dead prisoner was taken to the hospital. No one was permitted to attend to him.

Chapter 6

The Camp

THE PROCESSION of prisoners from the Theresienstadt transport was approaching the gates of Birkenau. At its end, Siegfried Lederer and Miroslav Zeimer walked with a group of children. From a distance they heard music. As they came closer they saw a prisoner band playing at the entrance of the camp. Are they playing for us? they wondered. Are they welcoming us?

Lederer did not know that in Birkenau and also in the whole complex of Auschwitz camps, music was being played for prisoners leaving for work. He saw endless columns of prisoners, marching in fives, passing by the watchtower. On a little platform in front of it stood the camp commander observing them. *"Muetzen ab"* (caps off), the Kapos shouted while marching past the commander, calling out the number of prisoners and the names of their brigades. The Blockfuehrers checked against their reports. Then the armed SS officers with their dogs surrounded the prisoners and led them to work, with their rifles ready to shoot. The prisoners passed the procession of newcomers from Theresienstadt and they could not believe their eyes. The brutal SS they knew so well had become gentlemen. They were consoling children, helping the sick, supporting the old, even a bearded rabbi. There was no cursing. The clubs, lashes, and rifles had disappeared.

Lederer and Zeimer were also surprised. They saw prisoners such as they had never seen before. Dressed in rags and tatters, instead of coats they wore paper cement bags. Hands without gloves, fingers stiff with cold. Feet in rags, boots held together by wire, dirty bowl-shaped caps covering their ears. A cart loaded with stones was pulled along. A fat prisoner with a green triangle on his coat sat on top. A ribbon on his sleeve bore the inscription Kapo. With a whip he urged on about a dozen skinny prisoners who were dragging the cart; they were yoked to it like horses.

The newcomers passed the women's camp next. Behind the barbed wire they could see creatures with shaved heads; they did not look like women at all.

Wherever they looked, the new prisoners saw oblong spaces fenced off by barbed wire. In each enclosure, there were two rows of wooden barracks standing close to each other. They looked like rows of carefully lined up coffins.

The procession passed through the open gates and the Theresienstadt prisoners found themselves inside the camp, behind the barbed wire fence. A wide road ran through the middle of the camp; at the end of it was a high watchtower. A machine gun on a turning platform could be seen at the top. Lederer counted sixteen barracks on each side of the road: long, dark green oblong huts with black tarpaper roofs. Instead of windows, there were only vents, instead of doors, gates.

The camp was busy. The newcomers and the friends and relatives who had been deported from Theresienstadt three months ago were together again.

"Siegfried, Siegfried!" somebody cried out joyfully, waving at Lederer. A smallish man in prison stripes embraced Lederer heartily. It was Otto Popel. He had grown very thin since the time the two men had worked together digging the mass grave in Lidice. Popel had a red ribbon on his sleeve with a white inscription: Blockaelteste (block elder). He took Lederer and Zeimer into the barracks.

"We exchanged the Sudeten barracks for stables," he said and opened the heavy door of their new home. There was little light penetrating through the small vents. When their eyes got used to the dark, they could see a narrow dirt path running down the center of the barracks. On both sides of it, along the entire length of the building, were primitive plank beds arranged in three tiers, one on top of the other.

"Here you won't find the comforts we enjoyed in Theresienstadt. We live, eat, and sleep on the bunks, and there are five of us to a bunk."

As they walked across the barracks Lederer counted fifty-four steps. The block was empty only a few sick lay here and there on the bunks. There were no cupboards or shelves. Some dirty rags were draped over the bunks of the sick. The air had a musty smell. A heating duct of red brick ran through the middle of the building, but in spite of the freezing cold it was not in use.

Popel took his guests to a little hut built of boards, which was separated from the rest of the block by a wooden bar. There was a small window, out of which the main gate of the barracks could be seen. Inside, there were three bunks, placed one on top of the other, a table made of unplaned boards, and two rickety wooden crates that served as chairs.

"This is the only private room here," Popel said, "and it is reserved for the Blockaelteste, their deputies, and their clerks. Now, everything is prepared for you. When we arrived in September, there was not even a road here. It rained for a whole week. We lost our boots in the mud. It rained into the barracks and we had nowhere to dry our clothes. There were no bunks and we slept on straw in the mud. Two hundred and thirty people died during the first month alone. This is a paradise compared to what it was."

The camp was like a beehive: the "old" inhabitants who found their relatives and friends wanted to live together with them. But the exchanges were suddenly interrupted by an order: *"Blockaelteste nach vorne!"* (to the front). Otto Popel rushed out.

After a while Popel came back to convey the order given by Rapportfuehrer Buntrock: "All those who have arrived today will occupy the empty blocks. They are not allowed to live with those who came in September. The men will live on the left side, the women on the right side of the road. The children will have a block of their own."

There was some grumbling and muttering, but nobody dared ask Buntrock for an exemption.

Soon, another order was heard: "Line up! Food is ready."

Pairs of men and women carried in buckets of soup. Each prisoner got a bowl of turnip soup and two pieces of bread. They had hardly finished eating when another order was heard: "All prisoners from the new transport line up immediately for registration."

Lederer and Zeimer waited in line for a long time. When their turn finally came, they were admitted into a hut. Ten prisoners with shaved heads and wearing striped clothes sat at a long table made of unplaned boards. A corpulent SS officer sat in a chair at the head of the table. He was the chief clerk of the camp's political department of the Gestapo. A number of forms, cards, a pen, and an inkpot stood in front of every prisoner-clerk.

In the corner of the hut, the prisoners took off their clothes and received the striped uniform in exchange. They were permitted to keep their underwear. At other tables their watches, wedding rings, pens, knives, cigarette lighters, cash, and other valuables were taken from them. The supervising SS officer examined everything carefully and put the things that appealed to him in his own pocket. Lederer noticed that they were allowed to keep their shoes. He gave a sign to Zeimer and they both hid their watches and knives in their shoes. The line at the clerk's table moved very slowly. It was long past midday when Lederer and Zeimer finally reached the clerk.

"Name?" asked a quiet, elderly prisoner. He wrote it in elegant letters on the top of a card. He filled in all the columns of the form, then turned to his supervisor and said, "A special case, Herr Scharfuehrer," and placed the form in front of the SS officer. The Scharfuehrer put on his glasses, glanced at the card, and ordered, "Step forward!"

Lederer stepped up and the officer said, "Are you a political prisoner? A Communist? A partisan? Speak!"

Lederer did not answer. He stood erect, holding his shoes in his hand. The Scharfuehrer examined the card carefully and then roared, "Arrested in 1939! Petchek House! Pankrac! Little Fortress! He was in every prison you can think of! And now he dares to come here, to this prominent camp! You have been lucky. But wait, we'll show you what's what!" He took his glasses off and scrutinized Lederer carefully.

Two prisoners in clean new striped clothes handed the SS two batches of triangles, one yellow and the other red, and a bottle of india ink. The SS Scharfuehrer took one triangle out of each pile and placed one on top of the other to form a Star of David. Over that he placed a strip of white linen with a number printed on it. He wrote the number on Lederer's card and added a note: "Dangerous: political."

Another prisoner-clerk handed Lederer four triangles and two linen strips with black numbers and explained to him, "Make two red-and-yellow stars out of the triangles. One to be sewn on the left side of your jacket and the other on the right side of your trousers. The two white strips are to be placed above the stars."

Another prisoner started tattooing Lederer's new name on his left arm: 170521.

The prisoners who had been deported from Theresienstadt occupied section B-II-b of Birkenau, which came to be called the Czech Family Camp. Compared with other camps in Auschwitz, the inhabitants of the Czech Family Camp had some unheard-of privileges. They did not have their heads shaved. They were allowed to keep their own shoes and underwear. They could, or rather they were urged, to write often to their relatives and friends. They were also permitted to receive food parcels from friends and from the International Red Cross. Families were separated, but they lived in the same camp and could meet without restrictions. This was not allowed in any of the other camps. The prisoner-doctors and nurses organized shelter for the old and sick in two of the barracks. The prisoners worked inside the camp only and were not forced to go out of the camp for hard labor. The children received larger food rations.

The Czech Family Camp also had a sort of self-government. The prisoners could appoint their own people for all duties except for the most important one: the Lageraelteste. For this function the commander of Birkenau, Schwarzhuber, chose a German criminal prisoner named Willy Brachmann. He had a weakness for alcohol and pretty women. There was plenty of both available. Willy, as he was called in the camp, could "organize," that is, he knew how to get what the SS wanted and thereby gain their favor. He also knew their language and was able to please even Rapportfuehrer Buntrock, dumb brute that he was. With a few bottles of brandy, Willy succeeded in persuading him to organize a soccer game instead of a boxing match, which was to qualify or disqualify the candidates for various camp duties. Eight block men were chosen from the winning team of eleven and nine deputies and clerks from among the defeated one. So it happened that Lederer got his block man's ribbon and Zeimer became his deputy and clerk of block no. 8. The block men's privilege was their hut. There they could meet with their friends. It did not take long for them to form a small group of conspirators. Its members were Lederer, Zeimer, Popel, Dr. Alfred Milek, and Ludvik Sand, the pharmacist. Later on, Fred Hirsch, a former member of the self-government group and a youth leader of Theresienstadt, joined as well. Hirsch succeeded in persuading Schwarzhuber to agree to permit the tutoring of children. The prisoners managed to establish a school in a stable, and the children decorated it with their own drawings. The outside of the school was in no way different from the other structures, but those who entered felt better immediately. On the walls were murals of fairy-tale scenes—Snow White and the seven dwarfs, Hansel and Gretel, and others. The children sang, recited, painted, read. Their teacher managed to create a little island of normalcy in the desperate atmosphere of the concentration camp.

Circulating among the prisoners of other camps were all sorts of rumors about the reasons for these privileges. While others lived under the shadow of gas chambers and furnaces, here was a family camp in the midst of the Auschwitz annihilation plant. They simply could not understand it.

Lederer's little group was also puzzled by the special privileges granted to the family camp. Its members were slowly gaining useful information about life in Auschwitz. The only people allowed to enter the family camp were members of the maintenance squad and sanitary and clerical workers. From them it was possible to learn about the secret resistance movement in other Auschwitz camps. Lederer also gradually learned about the mentality of the SS and the secrets of life in the camp.

One day, Soviet prisoners of war came to the family camp, accompanied by SS. They brought bread from the central food store located in the main men's camp B-II-d. They were cautious and would not speak to anyone. Lederer noticed that their wheelbarrow had a double bottom.

"That's how they bring bread and medicine from our comrades in the main camp," Dr. Milek, the prisoner-physician who worked in the hospital barracks, explained.

"How is that?" asked Lederer. "Aren't they hungry in the main camp? Have they bigger rations? And how about the SS officer who is supposed to watch them? Why doesn't he care?"

"You have to learn to 'organize.' Those who don't do it, won't hold out."

"Organize? What do you mean by that?"

"Get watches, diamonds, foreign currency, and you will get anything that is needed on the block," said Milek.

Lederer and Zeimer persuaded the "rich" of the block to give up their valuables for the benefit of the whole block. Up to now, prisoners were giving these things to Willy, in order to gain his favor.

After the arrival of the December transports from Theresienstadt, there were many more inhabitants in the family camp than before. The Soviet prisoners of war could not manage by themselves and so the block men and their clerks used to help them fetch the supplies. One day they went to the main camp and placed the wheelbarrow in the gate of the storehouse. The Soviet prisoners formed a chain and threw loaves of bread from the store into the wheelbarrow.

Lederer went to the SS officer who was supervising them and said, "Herr Scharfuehrer, I found a gold watch."

"Let me see!" The Scharfuehrer took the watch eagerly, looked at the markings, and counted the precious stones. While he examined the watch, loaves disappeared into the double bottom of the wheelbarrow.

Then the SS Scharfuehrer counted the loaves that he could see and added two more.

"That's for your find," he said to Lederer.

Before returning to his barracks, Lederer went to the hospital block, which was situated at the other end of the camp. Dr. Milek had asked him to bring some medicine from his colleague Dr. Cipera. The prisoner-physician was already waiting for him.

"Won't the 'organized' loaves mean you'll get smaller portions?" Lederer asked.

Dr. Cipera smiled. "Don't worry. We usually report deaths of prisoners a day or two late. The SS therefore receive food for those already deceased. They have enough extra supplies so that they can sell whole carloads of food in exchange for liquor, bacon, and cigarettes. We get some of it through the civilian workers who occasionally come to our camp. The boys from 'Canada' pay for it in hard currency."

The physician went to a small room, separated by a partition of boards, and returned with a few little boxes of Coramine vials, a syringe, and some needles. "This is for Dr. Milek," he said.

Lederer was shocked. "How did you get all this? Such precious things!"

"From the comrades in 'Canada,' " replied Dr. Cipera.

"How can they get them, and how do they know what is needed?"

"There are specialists in 'Canada.' During the selection on the platform, the SS ask everybody about their professions. The tailors, shoemakers, bank officials, goldsmiths, watchmakers, opticians, dentists, physicians, and nurses—these are professions that are in demand. Specialists are chosen to sort out and classify the belongings of the deportees. Then the things are sent to the Reich. The SS carefully supervise the prisoners of 'Canada,' but in spite of that, they manage to smuggle through what is needed. And remember, a good 'organizer' never carries the contraband in his pockets! Open your shirt and trousers!"

Dr. Cipera took paper bandages and laid out the vials, the syringe, and the needles in between them. Then he wound the bandage round Lederer's waist.

"It will fill the emptiness of your stomach and you will easily get by the SS checking the gate."

Rapportfuehrer Buntrock was on guard at the gate of the family camp. He stopped Lederer and searched his pockets. Lederer could smell the liquor on his breath.

"Proceed! But if I ever find anything, you are done for!"

Because of his big square head and swaggering gait, Buntrock was called "Gorilla" by the prisoners. He drank a lot and was the terror of the camp. When drunk, he liked to check up unexpectedly on what was going on in the barracks. Once he found a woman in the men's quarters at night.

"What are you doing here?" he shouted at her.

"I came to see my husband."

"Who is your husband?"

The woman had to go back past the bunks along the heating channel. She stopped at her husband's bunk bed. Buntrock followed.

"Out!" roared the Rapportfuehrer at the man. He ordered the woman to stand on top of the heating channel and her husband next to her in his underwear.

"What is she doing here?" Buntrock asked.

"She is my wife and she came to see me," replied the man.

"You lie, you dog!" yelled Buntrock and his eyes shone hatefully.

"She is a bitch and you want to screw her!" Buntrock took the whip he carried in his boot and beat them both until they fell on the floor. Then he kicked them, stomped on them, and roared, "I'll beat the hell out of you! You'll soon lose your appetite! You won't make a brothel out of this block!"

Rapportfuehrer Buntrock was dangerous even when sober. He watched the camp through his binoculars, spied on the blocks, and constantly called prisoners for interrogation. He thus kept the camp in a state of tension and fear.

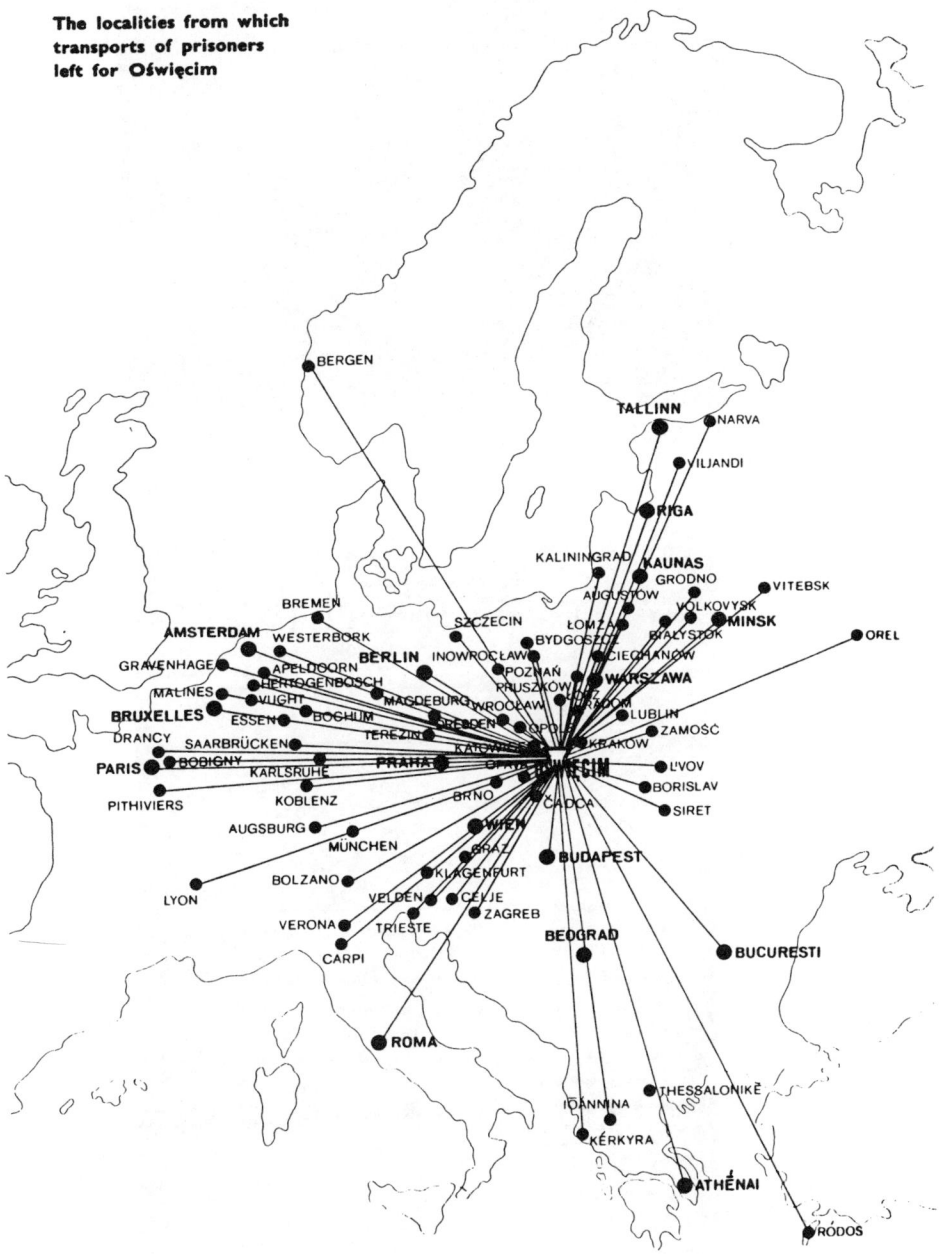

The localities from which transports of prisoners left for Auschwitz (Oswiecim).

SS Drs. Joseph Mengele and Bernhard Lucas

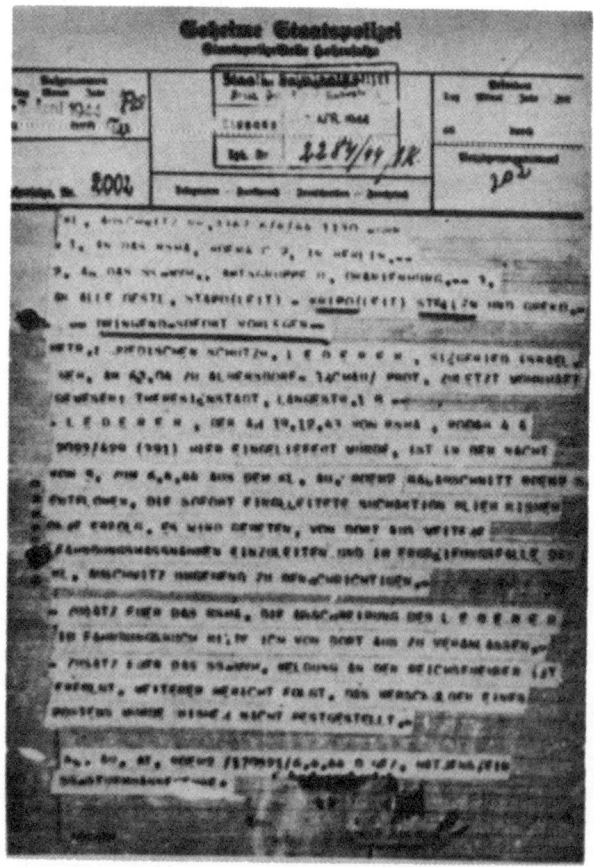

Gestapo warrant for the escaped Siegfried Lederer.

Siegfried Lederer

Siegfried Lederer (right) with a Russian partisan after the liberation in Plzen.

Massacred men of Lidice at the garden of Horak's farm, killed by SS men as a reprisal for the attack on SS general, Reichsprotecktor Heydrick, May 1942.

Life in the street of Ghetto Theresienstadt 1943–44

The inmates of the Theresienstadt ghetto leave the working barracks.

Food distribution in Theriesenstadt.

The camp of Auschwitz-Birkenau. The first row of barracks was the quarantine camp B-II-a from which the family camp inmates were taken to the crematoria. On the right can be seen the guarded border with deep water trenches, barbed wire fences, and guard towers with machine guns.

Arrival of a transport to the Theresienstadt ghetto 1943.

The arrival of deported Jews at the platform of Birkenau.

Chapter 7

René

THE ARRIVAL AT THE CAMP was a terrible shock for the two women who were entrusted to Pestek's care by Dr. Mengele. René's father, Ernst Karen, had been a rich and influential barrister in Prague. His wife and daughter had enjoyed an easy life. There was nothing they had wanted for. Dr. Karen, a very prudent man, had not waited for the authorities to close down his office. As soon as the Nazis came to Czechoslovakia, he sold his firm and used the money for organizing legal as well as illegal emigration for friends threatened by the Nazi persecution. But the Gestapo and Eichmann's Central Emigration Office soon found out about his activities. They wished to use Karen's connections abroad for blackmail and for gaining foreign currency. Keeping an eye on Karen, they let him continue his work for a whole year. They only summoned him to Gestapo headquarters for routine questioning. But when he was summoned for the third time, Karen collapsed.

René could well remember the day her father was brought home, beaten unconscious. It was Christmas 1941. Within an hour, both she and her mother had to leave their comfortable flat. The family of a

Nazi functionary from Berlin was already waiting in front of the door ready to move into their quarters. While René huddled with her mother in a maid's room fearing for Dr. Karen's life, the Nazi intruders celebrated Christmas, singing, "Stille Nacht, heilige Nacht."

Dr. Karen did not live to see the next day. René and her mother went to live with their aunt with the few belongings the Nazi occupants of their flat allowed them to take along. Six months later, they were summoned to the Jewish community center and sent to Theresienstadt.

Thus René learned the hard facts of life. But she was strong and determined to pull through. Her mother, however, was unable to cope with the situation. She got more and more apathetic. Her loving daughter was unable to help her. The journey to Auschwitz and the murder of Steiner, which she had witnessed, depressed her terribly. She was so upset that she attempted suicide. But the pills she swallowed were not enough to kill her. She only added to her daughter's sorrow. But René was a strong-willed girl and the harder the blows, the more determined she became to survive. She was heir to her father's fighting spirit. She was nineteen and knew that she was pretty and bright. She wanted to live.

Dr. Mengele's recommendation did wonders even in the chaos that prevailed in the camp immediately after the arrival of the Theresienstadt prisoners. Mrs. Karen was placed in a special section of the hospital barracks (where Dr. Mengele conducted his experiments on twins). The tattooing and registering was done while Mrs. Karen was lying in bed. Rottenfuehrer Pestek came into the block in the afternoon. He saw the patient and asked about her daughter. They brought the girl in. René stood shy and helpless in front of the tall, handsome officer. She recognized him as the SS officer who had taken care of them at the platform and guessed he was about twenty-two years old. Rottenfuehrer Pestek looked at her: fair hair, light blue eyes, beautiful complexion. He felt a strong attraction.

"To which block were you assigned, René?" he asked.

René was indignant. Who allows him to be so familiar? Why does he look at me like that? She took her time replying, "Block number seven."

"Have you any warm clothes?" asked Pestek, noting her soiled summer frock, which somehow did not seem to belong to her.

"They took away my coat and my dress and marked me like a piece of cattle." She rolled up her sleeve and showed the tattooed number on her arm.

"That's just for registration purposes. It doesn't mean anything," Pestek replied. He felt embarrassed and quickly left the room.

The "miracle" of the platform continued in the camp. René was soon moved to the "prominent" block. Instead of a straw sack, she got a real mattress. Then two woolen blankets came from somewhere. Instead of old rags, she had a nice gray skirt, a colorful shirt, a pullover, warm stockings, and shoes. The unknown donor also arranged for her to get two portions of food every day. She could share them with her mother. The cook and the Kapo storekeeper kept silent when she enquired where these came from. She thought, It could be only him, the tall officer from the platform, the one who had her called to her mother the other day.

Pestek often came to her block. His behavior was entirely different from that of the other SS. He always greeted them cordially, never shouted or cursed. During the block women's reports, he always looked at René. The last time he left he had turned back at the doorstep. René could have sworn that his "Good night" had been meant only for her. She saw him in front of her: tall, with his black eyes twinkling and smiling at the sight of her. He was always clean and looked sympathetic when facing the crowd of hungry and depressed females, in the midst of the dirt and odor of the barracks.

René was soon promoted to clerk of the block. She moved to a special hut, which she shared with the block women only. She got more clothes, underwear, some face powder, and even lipstick. She did not have much to do. She used to sit at the table in her room and keep a record of the incoming and outgoing letters of the prisoners.

Rottenfuehrer Pestek came often to her office, especially when he knew that René would be alone. He was a little embarrassed at times; he looked through the card index, took out some cards, and put them back again. Sometimes, as if by accident, he touched René's hands. She realized that she rather liked him touching her. But she could not ignore the skull and bones on his lapels. He was German and an SS Rottenfuehrer. Still, this German officer somehow did not belong to the concentration camp. She imagined him without his uniform, sitting on a school bench or running on a playing field. But she immediately scolded herself for being such a fool. He is SS and they are all alike. He chose his uniform deliberately, just like his colleague Rapportfuehrer Buntrock, the one with a head of an ape and the abominable, hateful eyes. She could not forget how Buntrock had frightened her when she had been forced to change clothes. It was someone like him who had beaten her father to death. Pestek is young and handsome; he knows how to make a good impression. But what would he do if ordered to torture and murder? Would he refuse? Hardly. He would be obedient and cruel just like the rest of them. At the same time she thought of what the girls on her block were saying. Maybe she could make things easier for herself and for her mother. If she only knew how. But she shuddered with disgust. No, she would have nothing to do with this SS officer, no matter how elegant and attractive he is. She would not let him touch her. She would refuse him if he dared make advances to her.

Viktor Pestek did not understand his own feelings. Once he had read a book about a boy and a girl who loved each other and promised to be faithful for ever and ever, even though they could not marry. But Pestek had never behaved like the boy in that book. He just took whatever was available. He was not choosy or particular. Girls liked him, and he occasionally enjoyed being with them, but he soon forgot the girl of yesterday.

But with René it was different. He caught himself thinking of her wherever he went. He thought about how pretty she was. He recalled how she combed her thick golden hair. He did not like his emotions—they made him feel uneasy. He was ashamed of himself for letting her get to him so easily. He was used to winning women's affections quickly and without difficulty. But this girl treated him like a little boy. Damn it all, it isn't normal, Pestek said to himself. Other girls would do anything to win my favor, but this one hardly answers me when I speak to her. She is not dumb. She must understand that there is a reason for her getting a clerk's post. She must know that the clothes and everything else didn't just come out of nowhere. I won't stand for it. I want to know how I stand with her, Pestek decided, and went straight to the seventh block.

He knocked, but opened the door without waiting for an answer. René was alone in the hut. His firm resolve vanished at the sight of her. He stood there with his cap in his hands and could not utter a word. René was enjoying his embarrassment, but after a while she looked at him in a friendly manner and said in a soft voice, "Shall I console you, or be sorry for you?"

Rottenfuehrer Pestek had no experience in talking to this sort of girl. He was used to saying what he thought, clearly and bluntly, sometimes even harshly. But René was different from the other girls he had known. She was superior to all of them. It was not only because of her beauty. It was her manners, behavior, and speech that were so striking. She was very gentle and yet she never said anything nice to him. He would have liked to have known why. But now he was at a loss; he did not know what to say.

"Why don't you call me by my Christian name?" he asked.

"People in our country do that only when they are good friends."

"I would like to be a good friend to you, but you do not trust me."

"Are you surprised? Look what you have done to us! Do you want me to forget my father, who was beaten to death, and my mother, who has become a wreck?"

"I know it's hard for you, René. I cannot change what happened. The only thing I can do is try and get you whatever is available here and help you to pull through until the war is over. It won't last much longer. Hitler is losing."

"Are you trying to provoke me? You speak as if you were not one of them."

"I don't sympathize with them," said Pestek. "Maybe it's because I did not grow up among them. My parents moved from Germany to Bessarabia when I was a little boy. They settled in a village near Czernovice. They had a small farm there. There were other Germans in that region, too. I often think of my four little sisters and of the green fields of Bessarabia. The farm was not big enough to support the whole family. I was sent to a blacksmith to learn the trade."

"And how did you get here?" René interrupted him eagerly and realized all of a sudden that she would be glad if he could find an excuse for his position.

"Everything changed when they dethroned the King of Rumania. Antonescu took over. He was a dictator and his Iron Guard made a pact with Hitler. The German colony in Rumania voted for the Volksdeutsche. Propagandists were sent from Germany. They promised a better life and recruited young men. I was drafted into the SS. I did not protest; I longed to see something of the world and I thought that this was my chance. But the big world shrank into a training camp. Instead of discovering how other nations lived, I learned about the horrors of the war. I was wounded by a grenade on the Russian front and taken to a Polish military hospital. The wound healed, but I was not fit for the front anymore. So they put me in another uniform and sent me to another training center. They drilled us from morning to night. It was meant to break our will; the discipline was cruel and we had to obey. When I came to Auschwitz I realized that I had lost my freedom altogether."

"Our fate seems to be similar, only you brought it on yourself by your own will," René said, full of reproach.

"Nobody cared about politics in our family. We lived only for the family and for our work. When the Nazis came, I did not have the slightest idea what I was getting into. My parents would be very unhappy if they knew where I am. I did not dare tell them, not even when I was home on leave."

René fingered Pestek's cap. "Still, you are with the victors. I am on the side of the enslaved and this is what is in store for me!" She pointed with disgust to Pestek's skull-and-bones emblem and looked into his eyes. "To make it clearer, they should have added a crematorium chimney. You can't deny that people are gassed and burned here!"

"It doesn't concern those who came from Theresienstadt," replied Pestek. "I don't know why, but you have privileges. The commander said you were under the protection of the International Red Cross. He gave special instructions for handling you."

"And you fulfill them as best you can," René said. She put the cap on Pestek's head and adjusted the angle in a rakish manner. Then she waved her hand toward the door; they had both heard the sound of a key turning in the lock. The block woman was returning. Rottenfuehrer Pestek quickly embraced René and kissed her. She did not resist.

Chapter 8

You Have Nothing to Lose

A YOUNG, FAIR GIRL was typing in a small office on the ground floor of the camp administration building. A tattooed number on her left arm disclosed her to be a prisoner. Her name was Klara Song and she came from Slovakia. Klara was an efficient typist and stenographer and could speak the language of the *Herrenvolk*. Sometimes she even worked as the telephone operator. Schwarzhuber could not find anybody more reliable and less expensive. He could not stand the rank-and-file SS in his office. "Fuehrer's best men belong to the front" was his opinion. He also did not consider the girls of the *Bund der deutschen Maedchen* (the Association of German Girls) to be suitable to serve where they would be in touch with the "most secret affair of the Reich." On the whole, he thought it best that his purebred fellow countrymen should not know much about his work. He was convinced that this was also better and safer for the Reich. He preferred to employ as many prisoners as possible since they could carry the secret only into the gas chambers, whereas the SS officers could carry it to the front. Those SS who knew too much and whose reliability came to be questioned by the political department of the Gestapo in Auschwitz were usually sent to fight on the front.

A light on the telephone switchboard panel went on. Klara Song got up from her typewriter, put on the headphone, plugged in the lead, and pressed the button. The commander of Birkenau had a call from the head office of the main camp, Auschwitz I. Klara pressed the button again and heard Schwarzhuber, who was in his office upstairs, take the call. Schwarzhuber recognized the voice of Commander Hess. He got up and repeated the received order.

"The six-month quarantine of the first Jewish transport from Theresienstadt will expire on the seventh of March. A *Sonderbehandlung** is to be carried out for all the prisoners from this transport on that date. Exceptions are possible for physicians and twins. Their names will be given to you by Dr. Mengele. It must be ensured that the special treatment is carried out smoothly."

Klara Song heard every word of the order. Her first thought was to warn the prisoners. She put down the receiver and loosened a fuse in the panel. The light went out.

Schwarzhuber shouted into the telephone excitedly. He knocked on the cradle and cursed. Then he ran down the stairs and opened the door of the office violently. Klara sat quietly at her machine typing busily. When he saw her working and composed, he calmed down somewhat. Nevertheless, he blurted out, "Why don't you take the telephone?"

When she told him that there was something wrong with the exchange, he ordered, "Have it repaired immediately!"

Klara went next door to inform the SS officer on duty. In a few minutes, the officer in the guardroom of the central camp called the Kapo of the maintenance squad through the loudspeakers: "Send some people to repair the telephone switchboard in the head office immediately!"

In a little while, two prisoners arrived. Klara knew them well. They were members of the Auschwitz resistance movement.

"You have to warn the people in the family camp," she said.

The entrance to the Czech Family Camp was guarded by the SS from a well-built, spacious wooden hut called *Blockfuehrerstube*. It was situated between the gate of camp B-II-b and the main road. The prisoner-plumber named Karel Krasa came to the guardroom window. He had on blue overalls with wide red stripes of oil paint on his back and on both sides of the trousers. He carried a kit by its leather strap.

---

* *Sonderbehandlung* (special treatment) was a Nazi code word for killing Jews in gas chambers.

He took his cap off and said, "Prisoner No. 73043 asks for permission to enter the camp."

Buntrock fixed his bloodshot eyes at the plumber suspiciously. He examined his pass and the tattooed number on his arm. Then he looked at the kit.

"Come in, my dear," he said derisively, pulling the prisoner by the strap inside the guardroom.

The plumber put the kit on the table and the Rapportfuehrer bawled out, "What's in there? What are you going to do in the camp? Looking for a slut, aren't you?" He threw all the tools onto the floor and inspected the bottom of the kit.

"I have been ordered to repair the pipes in the washroom," said Krasa calmly and produced the order signed by the SS technical department commander.

"All right, you may go." Buntrock had to agree, though he did not like it. "But I'll make it hot for you if I find you in a block!"

The washroom was located in a big barracks in the middle of the camp. Buntrock watched the plumber through his window with his binoculars. But Krasa knew it. He entered the washroom from the main road of the camp. He lingered a little when opening the gate and thus gave others an opportunity to see him. The washroom equipment was very primitive. Two rows of pipes, two inches wide, ran above wooden troughs. Water was turned on three times a day for short periods that hardly enabled the nine thousand prisoners to wash.

As soon as Krasa had turned off the main water valve and unscrewed the tap, Lederer, Fred Hirsch and Dr. Alfred Milek slipped in through the back door, which could not be seen from the guardroom.

"I have bad news for you," said Krasa after he greeted them. "An order for a 'special treatment' came today from Berlin. Schwarzhuber is supposed to liquidate all those who came from Theresienstadt by the September transport on the seventh of March."

"That's impossible," Fred Hirsch blurted out as if he had been bitten by a snake. "Only a fortnight ago a delegation of SS officers from Berlin headed by Eichmann came to see the camp. I know Eichmann from Theresienstadt. He talked to the children at the school, listened to their recitals, and took interest in their paintings. He praised them and gave chocolate to the best. He wanted to know what and how we teach them and then he said to me, 'Hirsch, write it all up for me. It's an interesting experiment. The distrustful gentlemen from the Swiss Red Cross should come here and see for themselves what we do for the education of Jewish children in the concentration camps.' "

Dr. Milek said, "Why should they distribute serum to vaccinate children against diphtheria? Why should they order isolation and treatment of typhus and dysentery?"

Lederer stopped them both with a brusque gesture. "Don't be naive. I know the Nazis well. They are cunning and ruthless. They'll do anything to deceive us." He asked Krasa, "Is there anything we can do?"

"We must not lose our heads. We can resist. Defend ourselves. We shan't give up without fighting. We talked it over in our camp and the boys think that if you see liquidation is really being prepared, you should set the straw sacks and bunks on fire. That will serve as a signal for a revolt in all the other camps."

"But how? And by means of what?" asked the others.

Krasa cautiously looked out through a peephole in the wooden wall. He saw that the road was clear all the way to the guardhouse. Popel had arranged for the back entrance to be guarded as well. He removed from his plumber's kit the pipes and the knee joints he had brought. Without a word he unscrewed and loosened the fittings. Petrol vials dropped out of them.

"Put these in your straw sacks. I suppose you have matches, haven't you?"

That was not all. Krasa unscrewed the long, hollow handle of a heavy wrench and took out small, thin bags of gunpowder.

"Make grenades out of that." He loosened the handle of a screwdriver, took out a piece of paper, and said, "Here are the instructions."

When he was about to leave, they all assured him that they would take his advice and get ready for the revolt. Yet Krasa felt that he had not managed to convince them that the danger was imminent. He was not quite sure whether they would find the courage and determination when the time came. He repeated, "Don't be deceived. The SS will not spare anybody. You have nothing to lose!"

In the evening, the members of Lederer's group talked the situation over with other prisoners. There were no moral or material conditions for a joint action in the camps of Birkenau. They had no arms. There was not enough gunpowder. This was smuggled in very small quantities from the Krupp munitions factory in Auschwitz. But there were plenty of petrol vials. These were "organized" by the prisoners of the clearing-up brigade out of the lighters of the newcomers. The only reliable allies were the prisoners from the *Sonderkommando* (special squad), who manned the gas chambers and furnaces. They were ready to set the crematoriums on fire as soon as they saw the fire signal from the Czech Family Camp. Then they would assault and fight the SS. They all had one thing in common: they had nothing to lose.

Chapter 9

Operation "Heydebreck"

ON MARCH 5, soon after the morning roll call, a command car drove into the family camp. It stopped in front of block no. 2, the block in which the administrative office of the camp and the post office were situated. Camp Commander Schwarzhuber and Dr. Mengele got out of the car and entered the office. A small, bald prisoner with glasses was sitting in the midst of boxes and cards; his name was Frank. He was the chief clerk of the camp. He got up and stood at attention, then quickly reported and gave an account of the numbers of each category of prisoners. Schwarzhuber checked him condescendingly; he wished to see the lists of transports. He was surprised to learn that out of the 5,007 prisoners who had arrived in Birkenau in September 1943, only 3,900 survived. Frank assured him that the numbers were correct.

Schwarzhuber turned to Dr. Mengele. "Over a thousand dead in half a year. Don't you think it's rather a lot for a prominent camp, Herr Obersturmfuehrer?"

"This only confirms our doctrine as well as the results of my research concerning the inferiority of their race," the physician replied confidently. Dr. Mengele was a member of the Research Institute for

Hereditary Biology and Care of the Race in Frankfurt am Main. There he sent the results of his experiments with twins and long scientific treatises worked out for him by the imprisoned physicians.

Buntrock entered the office. He reported that the block leaders had lined up. In front of the block, twenty block men stood together with their chief, the *Lageraelteste,* all dressed up. As soon as he saw the commander, Willy Brachmann ordered, *"Muetzen ab"* (caps off)! He reported to Schwarzhuber, who ordered them to stand at ease. For a moment, there was a slightly sly expression in Schwarzhuber's eyes. He tried to look kind but the traits of his face remained cruel and hard.

"Blockaelteste!" Schwarzhuber addressed the prominent prisoners in a soldierly manner. "I remember the time a half a year ago, when you arrived. There was but marshy land here and half-finished provisional huts. You managed to create a reasonable home in this wilderness. But the war continues. Our brave soldiers carry the burden of it. We need your help. We need to build a new camp for prisoners of war in Heydebreck. You are going to go there with your families."

He then turned to Willy and said, "Make a transport list of all the prisoners who came in September!"

Turning to Buntrock he said loudly so that everybody could hear, "The same privileges you had here will also be granted in Heydebreck. Every prisoner will get one tin of meat and a loaf of bread for the journey. The children a cube of butter each."

Lederer stepped forward and addressed the camp commander: "Herr Lagerfuehrer, we have two blocks of old and sick. They will hardly be able to work."

Schwarzhuber looked carefully at the audacious leader of block no. 8, but let Dr. Mengele reply: "Your patients will stay here with those who came in December. They will join you as soon as they recover. They will be well looked after. They are in this camp under the protection of the International Red Cross."

The name "Heydebreck," unknown an hour ago, stirred the gray life of the camp.

"Heydebreck? Where is it? What is it like there?" The word went from one to another, mysterious and uncanny, meaning something different to everyone. To the optimists, it shone like a star of salvation. The pessimists were distrustful and apprehensive. Many were afraid of the change; they did not want to exchange the familiar for something uncertain. The "September people" envied the "December people"; they would have a camp of their own. The "December ones" grumbled that the "September ones" would get out of this hell of crowded, unheated, smelly barracks. The tattooed numbers, however, made substitutions from one group to another impossible.

Dr. Milek called some of the block men who had met with Schwarzhuber to the back room of the hospital block. Milek reminded them of what he had heard from Krasa the plumber. Lederer, Zeimer, Popel, and Sand each had something to say. They all seemed to understand. They promised to put the petrol into the straw sacks and start a fire when the signal was given. Nevertheless, at the bottom of their hearts they were still hoping. Schwarzhuber's trick made them hesitant. Fred Hirsch, who was highly respected among the block men, did his best to help Lederer and Milek convince the others, but even he himself still cherished a hope: maybe he would be able to show the gentlemen of the Swiss Red Cross what could be done with children behind barbed wire. The display of their paintings on boards of the stable and the fairy-tale serials that adorned the walls of the barracks were admired also by the SS officers of all the Auschwitz camps.

In the afternoon, Irma Grese, an SS guard, came to the camp. She was very talkative and quite popular, even with the prisoners. She delivered to Willy the letters that had come for the prisoners. Then she unwrapped a card box full of clean postcards. She took one out and showed it to Willy. The sender address printed on the back read: *Arbeitslager Birkenau bei Neuberun, Hauptstrasse, Haus No.* . . .

She explained to Willy, "The prisoners are to fill in the number of their block. The date to be put on is the twenty-fifth of March, because the cards will have to be censored first and that will delay the posting. There are several thousands of them."

The camp was seething. "Heydebreck" became a threat, a puzzle, and a hope all at the same time. Between the blocks, behind the hospital, and in all the places where the SS could not see them, the prisoners stood and discussed their future. Those who knew about the planned revolt talked about it in the block men huts. Opinions varied, but most prisoners were against the revolt. Schwarzhuber had managed to deceive them.

The news about the gassing, the date of liquidation, and the planned rebellion reached even Buntrock. He interrogated Dr. Milek, Sand the pharmacist, and some nurses from the hospital block. He did not get anything out of them. But the suspicion remained. He reported it to the commander, who had already heard other reports of unrest in the camp. He knew that a lot depended on a smooth and successful execution of the order that came from Berlin headquarters. He did not want to exchange his warm place in Birkenau for military decorations and a heroic death on the eastern front. He decided to check the situation himself. Buntrock, Pestek, and Willy Brachmann would accompany him on a night inspection of the camp. He knew that at night he would have a better chance of surprising the conspirators.

René Karen woke up in the middle of the night. She heard the shouting: *"Torwache, Torwache."* After that there was cursing and the opening of the block gate. She hardly had time to put a blouse over her nightgown. Without knocking, block leader Willy Brachmann merrily opened the door of her hut. His eyes were glistening. Obviously, he had had too much to drink. A few seconds later the camp commander entered with two SS. One of them was Viktor Pestek. The block woman on the upper bunk was just awakening. René stood up and clumsily reported the number of women in the block.

Schwarzhuber's eyes widened. He was taken by René's uncommon appearance. She stood there, only half dressed, and for a moment he forgot all about his status as commander. He said to Pestek, "She looks like a typical Aryan beauty."

Schwarzhuber drew nearer and lifted up René's head. He looked into her confused eyes and asked, "What is your name?"

"René Karen," she replied meekly.

"That's not a Jewish name. Are you really Jewish?"

Schwarzhuber wished to see the mother. Buntrock brought the groggy, worried, disheveled old lady. She did not resemble René at all.

"Is this your daughter?" he asked.

"Yes, that's our René," she replied, not understanding what this was all about.

"Is your husband a Jew?" asked Schwarzhuber, expecting his theory about René being crossbred to be confirmed.

"Yes, but he died. He was beaten to death by the Gestapo," replied the frightened woman without thinking about the consequences of what she was saying.

The word Gestapo stirred Buntrock. The liquor had had its effect. He jumped at the trembling old lady, clutched her robe at her neck, throttling her, and beat the old lady's head against the wall, shouting, "Just remember with whom you had her! How many Aryans did you seduce, you old whore! Speak up!"

Mrs. Karen did not reply. She collapsed and lay unconscious at the base of the wooden wall dividing the hut from the bunk space. Buntrock did not allow René to attend to her. While Buntrock was raging, Schwarzhuber had carefully watched René. He had not seen such a beautiful woman for a long time. He wondered why he had not noticed her earlier.

He took a few steps away from her, looked at her profile, and said,

"No, you don't look like a Jewess. Take your clothes off! You have a splendid figure, you needn't be ashamed of it!"

René was horrified. She crossed her arms against her breasts. She looked from one man to the other. Then she fixed her desperate eyes on Pestek. She hoped he would do something. Or was he going to watch her be disgraced?

Pestek did not know what to do. He turned his face aside. He could not stand it; he could not look into the reproachful eyes of his beloved.

René looked at Buntrock and was stunned. She saw a raging beast in his bloodshot eyes. She drew nearer to Pestek and pressed her hands even tighter against her breasts. Buntrock knew that René appealed to Pestek and that there was something between them. He hated Pestek. He was not one of them. He had an Iron Cross, but was not as hard as a German should be. He was a Rumanian *Volksdeutsche* who had come here from the eastern front. This was Buntrock's opportunity. Now he would avenge.

He went to René, stood with his big feet apart, and roared hatefully, "Don't pretend to be coy. Hurry up, you bitch! Down with your rags!"

René was terrified. She could not think. She just kept her arms crossed and dug her fingers into her shoulders. Buntrock shot a giant hairy paw at her and tore her blouse off her body. René ran to a nook between the wall and the bunks and tried to hide her nakedness.

Pestek's first thought was to kill Buntrock. He opened the holster of his pistol and stared at the fat freckled nape of Buntrock's neck and at his shapeless apelike head.

Schwarzhuber realized that things had gone too far. He had come in order to see what was going on with Operation Heydebreck. The game with René had to be postponed until a more suitable occasion. Now he must not make any mistakes. Nor should he underestimate the rank-and-file SS, however primitive they were. Gentlemen in very high positions have finished their careers because of *Rassenschande*.*

"Rottenfuehrer!" Schwarzhuber said, turning to Pestek. "See that this woman comes to headquarters tomorrow. Dr. Mengele will identify the traits of her race."

And off he went.

Schwarzhuber continued checking the blocks. He did not, however, discover anything that would justify Buntrock's suspicions.

The next day, Lederer managed to send a message to Krasa the plumber: "Schwarzhuber ordered a shower in the sauna tomorrow for all who are supposed to go to Heydebreck."

---

*According to Nuremberg Laws, any intercourse between Jews and Aryans was forbidden and severely punished as *Rassenschande*—the shame of race.

Krasa's people in the main camp guessed it was a trick. On the other hand, Fred Hirsch thought it an indication that the transport was seriously being prepared. After some consultations, Krasa told Lederer, on behalf of the leaders of the Auschwitz underground, "As soon as the procession from the family camp starts toward the showers, three of our men will begin repairing a chimney on the roof of the guardhouse that can be seen from your camp. If the procession turns toward the gas chambers, our people will put a strip of white tin on the chimney. That will be the signal for starting the revolt."

Meanwhile, the block men in the family camp lined the women and children into groups that were to go to the showers together. They were allowed to take towels, soap, and blankets with them. The groups were waiting on the camp's main road, in front of the empty barracks. The doctors, nurses, and sick did not have to go. Dr. Milek gathered together those who stayed and knew about the revolt. He distributed the vials with petrol to them.

"The block men will also have to go to the showers, so we can't count on them. If the signal comes, we'll set fire to the straw sacks ourselves."

It was on March 6, 1944, past three o'clock in the afternoon, when the procession of Theresienstadt prisoners, guarded by an unusually large number of SS, walked through the gate of the family camp.

At the same time, three men of the maintenance squad began to fix the chimney on the roof of the SS guardhouse in the main camp B-II-d. They watched the road and anxiously followed the route of the prisoners walking to the showers. The prisoners went around the main camp, then through a small stand of birch trees where two of the four crematoriums were hidden, and finally they turned into the so-called sauna. It was a disinfection station equipped with real showers.

Two hours later, they were seen returning. The long procession of nearly four thousand men, women, and children was returning from the "sauna" by the same route. Some were wrapped in towels, as advised by the SS physician, to prevent catching a cold.

Schwarzhuber's sly, devilish trick convinced most of the prisoners that the rumors about their imminent annihilation were untrue. Those who had been determined to fight now became hesitant.

The next day, the prisoners of the September transport from Theresienstadt lined up with their parcels, blankets, letters, meat tins, and loaves of bread. The block men, with ribbons on their sleeves and with new blue caps on their heads, led the people of their blocks. Fred Hirsch led the children. They were carrying their copy books, paintings, and the toys they themselves had made.

Schwarzhuber, Buntrock, Pestek, Willy, and Gestapo officers from the political department examined the tattooed numbers and checked them against the transport lists. The "December people" were forced to go back to the barracks and were forbidden to leave the blocks. Nobody was allowed to say good-bye.

The column of prisoners started to move. They passed the gates of the family camp and turned right to the main camp road leading to the railway station.

After about a hundred yards they turned right again and passed through the gate of the neighboring quarantine camp, B-II-a. Nobody was surprised at that; it was normal for the transports sent to work in the Reich to go through the quarantine camp.

Very strict measures were introduced that night in all the camps of Birkenau. No one remembered anything like it. Walking outside of the blocks or even opening the vents was prohibited under penalty of death. Machine guns were placed in front of the entrances of the blocks. SS officers with dogs paced and watched all camps. The sentries in the watchtowers were doubled. The camp road and the danger line near the barbed wire fences dividing the camps were illuminated by searchlights throughout the night.

Chapter 10

Defend Yourselves!

THERE WERE SIXTEEN BARRACKS in quarantine camp B-II-a, which was located opposite camp B-II-b, occupied by Theresienstadt prisoners. The two camps were separated by only a barbed wire fence charged with electricity. Whenever there were not enough railway cars for transportation of the prisoners sent to work for the Reich, the prisoners were temporarily placed in the quarantine camp.

On March 7, Rapportfuehrer of the quarantine camp, SS Rapportfuehrer Joseph Krupanek, received an order to place the Theresienstadt prisoners into the six speedily evacuated barracks until they could be transported to Heydebreck. For the optimists, this was further confirmation that Schwarzhuber was not lying to them.

The barracks were very crowded. There was not enough room on the bunks, so some prisoners had to sleep on their luggage on the floor in the narrow space between the bunks. Families were separated, men and women were placed in different blocks. The prisoners were heavily guarded. Block men's huts were occupied by the Kapos and every second hut in each block was occupied by SS Blockfuehrers. The SS responsible for the order ensured that nobody would leave his block.

They also kept their eyes on the Kapos, who sometimes took overly harsh measures against prisoners.

The day after they moved in, the prisoners were already less enthusiastic about the transport to Heydebreck. They felt the burden of the strict *Blocksperre* (curfew). They kept asking about the transport: When will it leave? Why are they not allowed to go out of the blocks? Why are the children not allowed to see their mothers? The Kapos just shrugged their shoulders and the Blockfuehrers' only answer was, "It is forbidden!" The children cried, the sick needed attention; women who had food for the whole family in their luggage wanted to send some of it to their husbands and children, but they were not permitted. The functionaries of Theresienstadt were helpless. People in the blocks were getting restless. They knocked at the gates, which remained shut, and Kapos began to use their sticks.

The tension was growing in all the blocks. Rapportfuehrer Krupanek rang up headquarters to inform the camp commander of the situation and to request permission to use harder measures. Schwarzhuber decided to come to the camp personally, along with two SS physicians, Dr. Mengele and Dr. Lucas.

"Any violence will make the situation even worse," Schwarzhuber explained. "If you let the Kapos do what they want, there will be a rebellion. We can't afford a violent liquidation of the prisoners in the middle of the camp. The revolt could easily spread into other camps, and we do not have enough men to handle it."

Dr. Mengele agreed. He also managed to convince the most obstinate Rapportfuehrers, from divisions a and d, that the use of force would be counterproductive. He decided to go to the camp immediately to calm the Theresienstadt prisoners.

Dr. Mengele and Dr. Lucas walked along the prisoner blocks. The road was empty. They could see prisoners' faces in the half-opened vents. They heard the hum of the prisoners and the noise of their banging on the wooden walls of the barracks. They reached the end of the camp and entered the hospital block. Mengele ordered the prisoner-physician and his nurse to take medicine and medical equipment and to accompany him and his colleague on the visits to the prisoner barracks. As soon as the physicians appeared in the open gates of the barracks with medical supplies, the tension eased. Dr. Mengele was asked about the transport.

"The arrival of the railway cars has been delayed. The transport will depart in the evening," he explained.

Dr. Lucas said, "I heard that there are many sick among you. Those who are seriously ill will be transferred to the hospital block in the family camp. Naturally, they will not be able to go with the transport. The others can be attended to here and now. Whoever is ill, report!"

The prisoners were hesitant and confused. Many of those who earlier wished to be allowed to go back to the family camp now kept silent. They again began to believe that the transport to Heydebreck was their only chance to get away from the Auschwitz furnaces. They knew that they could hope to survive only as long as they could work. The Germans were badly in need of labor. By working it was possible to save one's life or at least to put off the danger of a violent death.

The medical staff registered the sick, while the prisoner-physician generously offered pills. Dr. Lucas ordered injections. "You have to be in good shape when you arrive in the new camp," he said. "There is a lot of work waiting for you there."

Fred Hirsch and his pupils were with other men in block no. 6, when Dr. Mengele arrived there. Hirsch repeated his request that the children be allowed to see their parents, the request that had been rudely refused by the Kapos.

"You must understand, Hirsch," explained Dr. Mengele, "that the order to leave may come at any minute. The transport lists are made up according to names and block numbers, and you will board the train in the order of those lists. A missing or displaced person will cause delay and confusion. You will all be in the train by night at the latest, and in Heydebreck by tomorrow morning. There you will all meet. Meanwhile even the children must endure it. You have an influence on them. Use it to calm them. When I think of our soldiers on the front and about the families in our bombed-out Fatherland I am really surprised that the commander treats you with such patience."

Before leaving, Dr. Lucas asked in every block once more, "Are there any people who are in need of medical attention?"

Dr. Mengele took the transport lists, read the names of the doctors from camp B-II-b, and asked them to step forward. He ordered them to go back to the family camp to get the medical supplies ready for the transport. Then he led away the twins from block no. 6. He explained that the twins would get special injections to be protected from illness during the transport.

The visit of the doctors had changed the mood of the prisoners. They were more relaxed and the Kapos and the SS ceased to be nervous. But it was Schwarzhuber who was more relieved than anybody else. His carefully prepared lies had withstood the test. Schwarzhuber, as well as Dr. Mengele, knew well what was at stake.

After the evening roll call on March 8, a car from headquarters drove into camp B-II-a. Kommandant Liebehenschel, Lagerfuehrer Kramer, and Oberscharfuehrer Boger from the political department of the Gestapo got out of the car.

Schwarzhuber reported, "The transport of the prisoners from Theresienstadt is ready for the departure."

The Kommandant gave the order to start the operation. Schwarzhuber ordered Rapportfuehrer Krupanek to gather all SS officers from the blocks. Then he said to them, "The transport will leave just as any ordinary transport that goes to work in the Reich. Quietly and orderly, in accordance with the transport lists. Prisoners are not to be beaten. Suspicious cases should be isolated and reported without delay. The prisoners may carry only their hand baggage."

The night was clear. An SS squad marched toward the quarantine camp armed with light machine guns and bristling Alsatians. It stopped at the *Blockfuehrerstube* (the block leaders' room). Their chief reported to the Kommandant, who then walked around the outer chain of guards and ordered the sharpshooters to take up positions between the watchtowers. The barbed wire fence charged with electricity was not always reliable; several times an audacious prisoner had managed to block the whole system with a pair of scissors. The rest of the squad entered the camp. Men with machine guns hid in the shadows between the barracks. Dogs, hungry and restless, growled.

A column of trucks was seen approaching on the main road from Auschwitz. The headlights illuminated the barbed wire, revealing the chain of guards and the position of the sharpshooters. The trucks stopped in front of the camp gate. Rapportfuehrer Krupanek gave a sign with a red lamp and they drove through the gate. The first truck backed up to the open gate of the third block.

Krupanek opened the gate and shouted, "Line up in fives and get in! You may take only small hand luggage with you."

There was a hum of disagreement and protest. Schwarzhuber had promised and repeated several times that they would be allowed to take everything with them. The prisoners hustled into the hall, trying to smuggle their luggage through. Krupanek ordered the Kapos to force the prisoners back into the barracks. Then only five prisoners were allowed to enter the hall at a time. The Blockfuehrer counted them, checked them against the transport lists, and crossed off their names. The tension grew again. These people, whose fate had been decided a long time ago, were now worried only about their luggage. They unpacked and repacked the food and belongings that they did not want to part with. They put things in their pockets, under their shirts, bundled them or hung them over their necks.

Rapportfuehrer Krupanek said, "Do not worry about your luggage.

It will go with you to Heydebreck in a separate railway car. Just mark your name and your number on it."

The Kapos counted people as they climbed onto the truck. Only forty prisoners were allowed in each truck. The prisoners of Theresienstadt were prominent prisoners and their privileges were to remain in force till the very end. They were to travel in comfort. The first truck left and another drove in. Ten more were waiting. There were about six hundred people in the block.

The prisoners tried in vain to learn the destination of the departing trucks. The wings of the gate blocked their view and nothing could be seen through holes in the canvas tops of the trucks.

The luggage prohibition renewed the prisoners' uncertainty. They did not know where the trucks were going, and that made things even worse. The tension grew and quickly spread from one block to another.

On block no. 6, Otto Popel was talking to Hirsch. "We have been deceived," he said. The Kapos stood at the entrance, except for two who walked on the brick heating channel in the middle of the block. They used their sticks on the prisoners who climbed up to the vents to see in what direction the trucks were departing.

Popel did not believe Schwarzhuber. The Scharfuehrer's strange smile betrayed the lie. Popel put the petrol vials in his luggage. Hirsch no longer argued. He had nothing to say and he felt that Popel was right. But when Popel suggested that they assault the Kapos and start a revolt, Hirsch answered, "I'd rather die than see the children slaughtered."

Popel suddenly felt guilty. Although he had warned his comrades, he should have tried harder to convince them. Now he knew that there was no hope and he was ready to die. He was not afraid of death anymore.

He jumped up onto the heating channel, pushed the two Kapos aside, and shouted, "We have been deceived. They are taking us to the gas chambers. Defend yourselves!"

The Kapos who were guarding the entrance rushed inside and beat Popel about the head with their sticks. The Blockfuehrer pushed them aside, took out his pistol, and shot Popel several times.

Rapportfuehrer Krupanek's whistle gave forth a piercing sound, and he shouted, "Whoever moves will be shot!"

The back and the front gates suddenly opened and machine guns were seen pointing into the block. The dogs snarled viciously. The Kapos dragged out Otto Popel, who was near death.

Rapportfuehrer Krupanek said to the Blockfuehrers, "The camp commander has strictly forbidden any shooting. Rough treatment of the prisoners has also been forbidden." He then ordered the block men of the family camp to line up.

Schwarzhuber didn't try to conceal his anger anymore. "Your colleague has gone mad," he said. "He endangered the lives of all of you. I am beginning to lose my patience. You don't deserve any consideration anymore. You are unable to restrain your own people."

"The people want to know where the trucks are going," said Fred Hirsch.

Schwarzhuber thought for a moment. Then he told Rapportfuehrer Krupanek to order the guards to lead the block men to the barbed wire fence, where they would be able to see the road. The block men of the family camp saw the trucks just as they were driving through the gate of the camp. The trucks turned to the right and drove alongside the quarantine camp. In front of the women's camp, near the main guardhouse, they again turned right, toward the Birkenau railway platform. The empty trucks were seen driving back from the same direction. They were returning quickly; the railway station was only 1.5 kilometers away from the camp. The prisoners of Theresienstadt were relieved. There was no reason to worry. The whole uproar was nonsense. To go to the crematoriums the trucks would have had to have turned left—that was the road the prisoners came back along the day before yesterday, when they returned from the showers.

In the meantime, another SS column arrived: more men with machine guns and motorcycles with sidecars. They were reinforcements sent from the main camp. The camp commander knew what was at stake. SS Reichsfuehrer Himmler personally ordered the whole operation to be closely followed from Berlin through teleprinters.

Schwarzhuber approached the block men and said, "Go back to your blocks and make sure there is no more trouble. I'll stop the transport immediately if there is the slightest sign of unrest."

He turned to Hirsch and said, "I shall investigate who instigated the rebellion. If the culprit is not found, everybody in the block will be shot."

The information brought back by the block men convinced the prisoners. They had seen with their own eyes the trucks driving to the railway platform and soon returning empty. The prisoners of Theresienstadt now climbed onto the trucks without protest or delay. Those who had not yet marked their luggage did so as quickly as they could. They wished to get away from the hell of Birkenau as soon as possible. They were looking forward to being reunited with their families.

It was three o'clock in the morning when the last women and children left the camp. The Kapos then broke into the empty barracks and started to search the luggage.

Kommandant Liebehenschel did not utter a word during the whole operation. Now he tapped Schwarzhuber's shoulder and said with appreciation, "My congratulations, Untersturmfuehrer. Your last trick was decisive. It was risky, but it was worth more than a machine gun squad. I am going to report it to the SS Reichsfuehrer."

Schwarzhuber's smile was sly and self-confident. His tricks had worked. None of the prisoners knew where they were being driven to. He had managed to fool all of them.

But about that, Schwarzhuber was mistaken. Fred Hirsch knew that behind the railway platform there was a road that turned right to the crematoriums. Only when the truck drove past the fence of the women's camp, however, did Hirsch fully realize what was going on. But by then it was too late to organize resistance. He knew that by warning the prisoners he could achieve nothing but panic and slaughter. But neither did he want to accompany his beloved pupils to death. Instead of Zyklon, he chose Luminal.

Chapter 11

Twelve Minutes, Eight Seconds!

THE TRUCKS PASSED the rails and the railway platform. They entered through the big iron gate into a yard enclosed by barbed wire fencing. Strings of flickering bulbs, hanging from the tops of high, curved concrete pillars marked the borders of the camp. The brakes screeched. The first Opel-Blitz stopped near the dark outline of a crematorium. The prisoners began to jump off the trucks. Their eyes were blinded by the sharp glare of searchlights. Reflectors illuminated a short stretch of the road leading to the iron railings along the crematorium. The path was sprinkled with sand and lined by a dense column of fully armed SS guards in helmets. Their submachine guns glittered in the darkness from the reflected lights.

The prisoners of Theresienstadt descended the wide, concrete staircase into a large, whitewashed underground hall with concrete pillars. There were benches all around. Numbered pegs hung above them. Through an open door showers could be seen in the next room. There were signs with arrows, and the legend *Zum Baderaum* was supposed to reassure everybody that this really was a bathroom.

The prisoners were admonished, "Remember the numbers of your pegs so as to find your things after the bath!" But this trick, which had so often proved effective and even soothing, today became a challenge. The prisoners of Theresienstadt realized that they had been deceived. They knew they were about to lose their lives.

A battle broke out in the hall. With their bare hands the men of Theresienstadt assaulted the SS guards. The SS beat them with the prisoners sticks and forced them to undress. Every ten minutes another forty men came in another Opel-Blitz. A crowd of confused, blinded people were rushed down the staircase into the hall. The defenseless men, crowded into the small space, fought desperately. The SS expected it. They used the butts of their guns and smashed the prisoners' heads; with blazing flamethrowers they forced them into the *Baderaum*.

The prisoners, beaten and bleeding, were jammed into the gas chamber. Then suddenly the moaning stopped. The Czech national anthem, "Kde Domov Muj?" (Where Is My Home?), could be heard from the gas chamber. First, only a few voices; soon, some more; and finally, a great, solemn hymn, full of longing and rebellious gloom.

That's how Filip Mueller, the stoker in the crematorium, saw the prisoners of Theresienstadt for the last time.

While the desperate fight was going on underground, an ambulance marked with the Red Cross emblem stopped at the entrance of the crematorium. Two uniformed men got out. The first was elegant Obersturmfuehrer Mengele. He descended underground by the same path as the prisoners. The second man wore a uniform of coarse cloth. His cap lay at an angle on his square head. He was the "disinfector," SS Scharfuehrer Josef Klehr. He took five gray-green tins out of the back of the car and climbed up to a low, grassy slope that camouflaged the ceiling of the gas chamber, which was higher than the yard. Disinfector Klehr put his gas mask on. He released the lids of the tins by means of a round, toothed key. The inscription on them read: *Zyklon B Tesch und Stabenow, Gessellschaft fuer Schaedlingsbekaempfung, Hamburg.* He poured the contents of the tins into the shaft openings. The small green crystals fell through the hollow opening of the pipe.

The poisonous hydrocyanic acid seeped through the grating into the "bathroom" space. It choked and tore the lungs, split and decomposed the blood cells, and finally killed mercilessly.

While the disinfector was sealing the concrete valve, the chanting could still be heard: *"Mezi Cechy domov muj"* (Among the Czechs, there is my home). The sounds of another song echoed from the other shaft. There, as the people parted with life, they sang a Hebrew song,

"Hatikvah" (Hope).* On the threshold of death, they protested against a crime that no reprisals could avenge, no love redeem, no friendship forgive, no law punish. It would not be forgiven until the end of the world.

An SS officer stood at the massive metal-sheathed door in the basement. It was Dr. Mengele, a member of the Research Institute for Hereditary Biology and Care of the Race in Frankfurt am Main. Through the airtight peephole in the door, he attentively followed his victims' final struggle for life.

The commander of Birkenau, Johann Schwarzhuber, stood next to him with a stopwatch in his hand. As soon as Mengele lifted his head from the peephole, Schwarzhuber clicked the watch and declared, "Twelve minutes, eight seconds!"

Mengele turned the pages of his notebook; on the page marked "*Sonderbehandlung*, 8 March 1944," he marked the time given by Schwarzhuber. Then he said casually, as if he were timing a swimming contest, "It took two minutes more than it should. The pharmacist Capesius used a tin less of Zyklon than he should have. There were the children, too, and they resist longer than the adults."

Schwarzhuber turned to a group of prisoners standing behind the cordon of the armed guards and ordered, "*Sonderkommando* to work! Ventilators switched on!"

In Auschwitz-Birkenau's four extermination complexes (equipped with forty-six furnaces and eight gas chambers) this happened several times a day with unfailing accuracy. It was part of the secret "gas war." For these crimes the Nazis had a name of their own. In their secret papers, they called them *Sonderbehandlung* (special treatment).

A secret organization of prisoners had been sending information abroad about the meaning of this term. Nevertheless, people in New York, London, and Paris could not imagine what was really happening when they read, "Thousands of people are being destroyed in the extermination camps in the east." For two years, the secret couriers had carried this information to and fro. Nevertheless, there was not a single sign of reaction. Nothing had been done, no measures taken against these crimes. Who would inform the world about the murder of the Theresienstadt prisoners?

At the end of the main camp, a hut stood between two blocks in an enclosure that served as a dump for various building materials. Inside there were clamps, an anvil, a field furnace, and some tools and equip-

---

* "Hatikvah" became the national anthem of Israel.

ment that hung on the walls and lay about on the tables. The spacious railway station, with its three platforms, could be seen from the yard behind the long lines of barbed wire. The rails of the railway junction leading out of the Auschwitz station to Birkenau widened into three tracks. The side tracks separated the two sections of the camp and the rail ended between the crematorium buildings number 1 and 2.

The locksmith's shop was the only repair facility in the main camp. The artisans from there went daily to other Birkenau camps and repaired all the equipment necessary. The fire of the furnace, the noise of the hammers, the drilling machines and files—all served also as a cover for meetings of the members of the resistance movement. This particular night everything in the shop was unusually tidy. They were waiting for an order from the *Sonderkommando* from the block that had the worst guards and was separated by a wall and barbed wire from the other thirty-one barracks. There lived the prisoners who were forced to do the most dreadful work of all, the worst that can be imagined—to tend the gas chambers and crematoriums. Long after the evening roll call, a dark figure jumped down from the wide wall that surrounded the *Sonderkommando*. A prisoner in striped clothes sneaked along the front of the blocks toward the gate of the yard at the end of the camp. He shifted a loose lath in the gate and squeezed in. Then he straightened and walked through the short yard. The door of the locksmith's shop was unlocked. He entered.

Filip Mueller was a young student when he was driven away from his parents' home in Sered in the spring of 1942. When he came to Auschwitz, he soon learned what was going on. The Soviet prisoners of war were masters at escaping from the camp. They could deceive the SS and find help and connections in the countryside. Mueller wanted to know how they did it, so he made friends with them.

Once, three fugitives were caught far from the camp. The men returning in the evening from work saw them standing on a little step near the main gates, ragged, tortured, with a sign hanging from their necks: *Halo, ich bin schon wieder da!* (Hello, here I am again!) Later, they were hanged. Mueller was questioned about their escape attempt. On the way to the interrogation, he was told by the commander, "You should be hanged, because it is suspected that you intended to escape, but you will work before you die. You are young and inquisitive, so you shall go to the *Sonderkommando*. There you will learn a lot."

In the crematorium Filip Mueller fueled the furnace, burned the bodies of the gassed, and thought of how to escape. In the special brigade, they were all preparing for rebellion. They armed themselves.

They learned how to make Molotov cocktails. The gasoline was "organized" from the trucks. Women who worked in the Krupp-Weichsel-Union fuse factory in Auschwitz smuggled the gunpowder through various clandestine methods to the crematoriums. Filip took note of all the important events. He also brought news of the latest Nazi crimes, those that were supposed to remain secret, that the world was not meant to know.

The eyes of the three "specialists" who had repaired the chimney and roof gutters of the guardhouse three days before were now fixed on the face of young Filip Mueller. He related what he had seen.

"They quickly took us away from crematorium 1, where the men of B-II-b were liquidated. They were probably afraid that we would join them. I was working in crematorium 2, where the women and children were undressing. They went where the arrows and signs led them, to the 'disinfection and bathroom.' Some were still confident. They tried to cover the children to prevent them from catching cold. Those who realized what awaited them refused to proceed and wailed loudly. When persuasion and reproof did not help, they were taken by SS guards through a narrow passageway to the execution hall. There they were shot with a silenced pistol.

"The small children were frightened by all this, and they started crying. They were held by their mothers, but still they wouldn't calm down. The SS guards were real sadists, chosen for this quality. They were waiting for their opportunity. We wanted to prevent the worst and save the women from seeing their children tormented. We helped them. Many realized what was in store for them, but they consoled the crying children. We brought some toys. The children started playing and teasing, and many entered the gas chamber with a toy in their hands.

"It was more than I could bear. It was worse than the sight of the piles of twisted, dirty bodies when the door of the gas chambers opened. The commander, who wanted the 'special treatment' to be done as quietly as possible, urged us to console the women in the 'bathroom.' I used the opportunity and sneaked in with them to the gas chamber. On the threshold I saw a beautiful little girl with a yellow ribbon in her dark curls. She suddenly extended her arms like a butterfly and started to dance, carefree and gracious. She danced so beautifully that for a moment everybody forgot the horrors of death. Even some of the SS seemed touched. But the fairy-tale illusion in front of the gate of death did not last long. The commander of crematoriums, Chef der Verbrennerung SS Hauptscharfuehrer Otto Moll, was coming down the stairs fully armed, shouting, 'This is not a theater stage! No acting or ballet dancing! To the bathroom! *Marsch!*'

"The mother took her naked little girl by the hand and I led her to the open door of the gas chamber. Near the entrance the woman saw Schwarzhuber. He knew her from the family camp office. Even he seemed to be touched by the little girl's performance. The woman approached and begged him, 'Please, let the child live, she is innocent.' But Schwarzhuber remained unmoved."

Filip stopped for a moment and lit another cigarette. Nobody uttered a word. The stoker continued: "Two young girls guessed what I intended to do in the gas chamber. They came to me and asked, 'Why do you want to die when you can live? Is it not enough that we have to die? We want to live, but we can't! You stay alive and tell the world what happened to us. You can avenge our death!' And they pushed me out of the gas chamber, which was already nearly full. They kissed me on the threshold of death, and one of them put a piece of paper into my hand."

Filip unfolded the paper. There were three poems written on it: "We Are Dead and Accuse," "A Foreign Tomb," and "I'd Rather Perish."* They were written in a small, neat, female hand, but were unsigned. The author of the message sent out of the death chamber remains unknown.

That night the men in the workshop wrote it all down. It was a report of the biggest and most dreadful mass execution in the history of the Czech Jews. One copy was put into a watertight tin and buried. The other was delivered to the resistance leaders in the main camp. Karel Krasa put the third into the hollow handle of a screwdriver.

Viktor Pestek, unwilling participant in this vile crime, was deeply shocked. His determination to kidnap and save René intensified, and he tried to interest some experienced Jewish prisoners in his escape plan. First he tried to sound out the only Jewish Blockaelteste in the Birkenau men's camp, Ernst Rosin, who refused. He repeated his escape offer to the Blockschreibers, Alfred Wetzler and Walter Rosenberg.** When they asked him why he was willing to take such a risk, Pestek replied, "Because I hate to have to watch women and children being murdered." This was not enough to convince these cautious prisoners, who were aware of the past treachery of other SS.

Then Pestek turned to the Slovak Jew Josef Neumann, Kapo of the

---

* These poems were smuggled out of the camp in July 1944 with the help of the Czech civilian workers Moravec and Marak. They were published in Kulka and O. Kraus's book *The Death Factory* (Oxford: Pergamon Press, 1966), pp. 210-12.

** Wetzler and Rosenberg escaped to Slovakia from Birkenau on April 10, 1944.

Leichenkommando (the squad that collected corpses). Neumann's task was to visit all the Birkenau camps every day and determine how many had died in the last twenty-four hours. A handcart would be brought and the corpses transported to the mortuary outside the camp. Now, shortly after about four thousand members of the Czech Family Camp had been killed, Pestek contacted Neumann in the mortuary.

"You can see the danger you are in. Isn't what has happened to the Czech Jews enough? What do you think you will be able to do when the catastrophe strikes the other camps? How will you save yourself then? Make up your mind. Let me get you out of here!"

Pestek proposed that Neumann hide Pestek's Jewish girlfriend among the corpses in the handcart and pass through the camp gate when Pestek was on duty there. The cartload would then be brought to the mortuary, where Pestek would prepare an SS woman guard's uniform for René. "Then," Pestek promised, "I will lead you both safely out of the camp."

Neumann confided Pestek's offer to his friend Rosin,* who warned him against it, and cited a number of cases where dealings with the SS had ended in disaster. At the next meeting with Pestek, Neumann argued that his escape would compromise the lives of his sister and other relatives in Birkenau.

After repeated failure, Pestek made up his mind to search for an ally among the prisoners in the isolated Czech Family Camp.

---

* Rosin escaped to Slovakia from Birkenau on May 27, 1944.

Chapter 12

We Shall Escape in Uniforms

TWO PRISONERS WERE DIGGING a flower bed in the family camp in front of block no. 8. What they really were doing was watching a stretch of the camp road. In the block hut, the block man and his deputy were sitting at a wobbly table. Both Lederer and Zeimer became very agitated as they read the message that Karel Krasa had brought from the main camp. They followed the route of the trucks to the crematoriums on a primitive little diagram on which the route was marked in red. The route had been chosen so as to deceive even those who looked from the skylights and could have sworn that they had seen trucks driving from the quarantine barracks to the railway station.

"We must escape," said Zeimer. "There is no risk in it. We are just living corpses anyway."

"There you are mistaken," replied Lederer. "There is more at stake than our lost lives. It is necessary to find reliable means of saving thousands of lives here and many more outside. Hundreds of thousands of people live in their homes, hundreds of kilometers away from here, and none of them suspect that death awaits them here. No one in the whole world has the slightest idea of what is happening here in Auschwitz."

"It's all very well to escape," said Zeimer, "but what you need is somebody to help you when you get out. Partisans. The Russians know how to do it. They just disappear. The siren goes, but they are gone. It's just like sinking through the floor."

Lederer said emphatically, "I think it should be possible to get to Prague and sit there with a cup of coffee by the time the siren goes off here in Birkenau."

One of the prisoners who had been watching in front of the block came in unobtrusively and reported, "A messenger came to say that the block man is to report to the guardhouse immediately."

Lederer nervously fingered his hair, then examined his pockets and put the contraband on the table: cigarettes, a knife, a lighter, a watch. Then he put the blue cap of a block man on his head.

"Well, Miroslav, I am going. Should anything happen, stick together with the boys from the workshop!" Lederer left without saying goodbye. He thought of a thousand different things as he ran the 200 meters to the gate.

He knocked at the guardhouse door. Not a sound was heard. He slowly, reluctantly opened the door. Suddenly he realized that there was nothing to be afraid of. It was not the fearful Buntrock who was sitting at the table, but Rottenfuehrer Pestek, who was called "darling" because of his peaceful nature and boyish smile.

Lederer took his cap off and stood at attention as he reported himself. Pestek examined a card lying on the table. Then he looked up, scrutinized Lederer, and read from the card, " 'Treasonous behavior, a group sabotage in Pilsen, an attempt to escape. RU, return unwanted.'

"In general, you've seen too much. That's enough. I will take you tomorrow to the main camp in Auschwitz."

Lederer grew very pale. He did not expect this. Birkenau was supposed to be the worst. Worse than a bullet in your head or a rope around your neck.

Pestek observed the change in Lederer's face and asked, "Do you know where I will take you?"

"I can imagine. An interrogation bunker and a chop on the neck," replied Lederer, trying to be calm.

Pestek didn't say anything for a while. He wrinkled his forehead and pushed forth his lower lip. He had something on his mind.

"I'll tell you something," he said after a while, "but you mustn't open your mouth about it," and he pointed to the pistol lying on the table.

Lederer's eyes sparkled. He was anxious to hear what Pestek wanted to say.

Pestek continued, "If you ran away to Bohemia, would you find anybody there to help you? Would any of the members of that sabotage group cover you?"

Lederer hesitated. He did not know what to say. Was it a trap? Should he swallow the bait because of this nice, sympathetic face? Should he say something that even the Gestapo could not get out of him by beating and torture?

Pestek watched Lederer's face intently. Lederer kept silent.

"You have nothing to lose," Pestek said, interrupting the silence. He got up, went to Lederer, handed the card to him, and pointing at the letters in a red circle, he said, "Anybody who is RU is more or less dead. If you tell me the truth, I might give you good advice."

Lederer was thinking hard. Should he stake everything on one card and place himself at this SS Rottenfuehrer's mercy? It was true that Pestek was different than the other SS in the camp. People spoke well of him. He said to himself, I have nothing to lose and an opportunity like this might never come again. He had made up his mind.

"I have good and reliable friends in Bohemia," Lederer said. "They will help me."

"All right then. You have been called to the Gestapo. They will try to get information out of you any way possible. They will let you live as long as you don't speak. Report to me tomorrow at eight o'clock in the morning."

They started after the morning roll call. Pestek walked five steps behind Lederer, with his pistol cocked to shoot, according to the rules. For the first time Lederer was leaving the family camp. He remembered the little diagram of B-II-a, and now he tried to trace in his mind the route the trucks had taken from the quarantine barracks to the crematoriums that fatal night in March.

They turned right at the end of B-II-a, near a high, empty guard tower. Then along a barbed wire fence that bordered the second section of the Birkenau camps, and further along the main guardhouse. When they came to the place where the rails crossed, the road leading from the Auschwitz railway station to the crematoriums, they turned left. There about 2 kilometers of an even road could be seen, leading over a railway bridge to the town of Oswiecim (Auschwitz). The road slowly rose to the iron bridge that crossed two rail lines. Behind the bridge these branched off into the wide tangle that was the Auschwitz railway junction. A couple of rails went to Birkenau.

On the bridge they met an SS Scharfuehrer riding a bicycle. He stopped them, leaned his bicycle against the railings, arranged the silver cord that hung from his shoulder, and spoke to Pestek, who showed him an envelope. While the Scharfuehrer examined the papers, an express train passed under the viaduct and stopped with a noisy squeaking and creaking in the Auschwitz railway station. Lederer gazed at it, not believing his eyes. To him it was as if from another planet. Civilians could freely get on and off the train on the Auschwitz platform, while less than 3 kilometers away, that hell of Hitler's sat behind the barbed wire fences.

The Scharfuehrer with the silver cord asked Lederer to roll up his left sleeve. He examined the tattooed number, compared it with the papers, and then allowed Pestek to proceed.

Pestek had not spoken before, but now he said, "These flying *Sonderdienste* [special service men] are very dangerous."

When they passed the slope of the bridge, they turned right and went on to the main camp, Auschwitz I. There was a big gate with large iron letters on it: *Arbeit macht frei* (Work makes you free).

The guard took the prisoner and the papers from Pestek, lifted the red-and-white barrier, and led Lederer to a long, wooden barrack through a street of single-story, red-brick blocks. Lederer read the sign: *Politische Abteilung* (Political Department).

The guard made Lederer stand near a door in a row of prisoners with his face turned to the wall. Crying and shrieking was heard from within, and every now and then a beaten, bloody prisoner came out the door.

Lederer was not a novice. He knew what to do. He knew that the Gestapo were less brutal when they heard a prisoner speak their language well. He remembered back to when he was a boy and had often gone over the frontier to Bavaria, where he learned German at his relatives' house. Later he stayed with his uncle. It made things easier for his parents, who had three other children to look after. He spent several years in Bavaria when he was young; there he had experienced the pleasure and joy of his first love. He had considered settling in Germany for good, but when he saw the SS beat his uncle and aunt, the shock was enough to make him return home to the village of Alber. A year later the whole family fled to Plzen to evade the brown-shirted pestilence. His mother did not survive the shock. She died before the Nazis occupied the rest of Bohemia. Lederer had seen and experienced personally what the Germans could do. He knew he was not safe and looked for other courageous people with whom to join forces. He found them in Colonel Weidman's group.*

Plzen was an important place to the Nazis and one in which they were particularly vulnerable. Acts of sabotage at the Skoda Works, if well performed, were worth several squadrons on the front. Unfortunately, Lederer was found out and the Gestapo seized him at the end of the year. He learned who had denounced him when questioned in the Petchek house** by Commissar Rhode. From the cell in Pankrac he was taken to the Little Fortress in Theresienstadt and then to the ghetto. He was to be transported. In the ghetto he learned what had happened to his family. His father and sisters had been sent by direct transport from Plzen to the east.

Lederer then thought of the "good" times, when he was one of Holzer's firemen. He remembered the mass grave of Lidice and the death of Rudolf Steiner. He also remembered what the SS officer with glasses had said when he was tattooed: "We'll make it hot for you!"

At that moment, he had to stop thinking of the past. His number had been called. He entered the room and reported.

An SS Scharfuehrer with a square-shaped head and bristly hair sat at a big table. On the table lay a pistol, a whip, and a cat-o'-nine-tails. It was the same old story: Lederer's work in Weidman's resistance group. His interrogator read the record provided by the Prague Gestapo. Lederer denied nothing and, when questioned further, admitted that Rudolf Steiner had supported the group in Plzen.

The commissioner asked, "Do you know that Steiner had a daughter who was a crossbreed?"

"Yes, I do, Herr Scharfuehrer."

"What is her name?"

"Gitta Steiner."

"Where does she live?"

"In Theresienstadt."

"How do you know that?"

"I saw her there."

"You lie, you swinedog!" roared the officer and lashed Lederer's head with the whip.

"Where did he hide her? Speak!"

"I do not know. I saw her in Theresienstadt," repeated Lederer, who was bleeding now. After several minutes more of this, the com-

---

* An account of the history and importance of the Weidman group is given in the book *Pred dvaceti lety* or *Twenty years ago* (Prague: Nase Vojsko-SPB, 1965), page 35.

** The Petcheks were wealthy Czech Jewish industrialists. After the Nazi invasion their mansion was turned into the main Gestapo interrogation and torture facility in Prague.

missioner realized he would get no further information from this man. He took him to a small room; there, a prisoner, rattling in agony, hung from the ceiling by a chain bound round his wrists.

Another prisoner's blue and bleeding thumbs stuck out of a press. He had a gag in his mouth to keep him from screaming.

"I have no more time for you today," the Scharfuehrer said, "but I bet you will be able to recall everything next time we meet." He kicked Lederer out of the room.

Lederer stood at the other side of the gangway among the branded men and waited to be led away. No, he did not want to come back here. He already knew what these "investigations" were like. He had a souvenir from such an investigation.

In early 1940, soon after he was taken into custody, they took him to the Petchek house with five other members of the Weidman group. They questioned. They promised. They confronted. They threatened. The most obstinate men were taken to Chief Commissar Rhode's division. Lederer's turn came. An SS officer sat in a comfortable position at a big desk. The room was paneled in mahogany, the door upholstered, a thick carpet covered the floor. An SS guard sat near the white door. The officer behind the desk was looking through Lederer's papers; he waved Lederer to a chair in a friendly manner.

"Look here, Lederer," he said, his voice as sweet as honey, "you lived among us for a long time in Bavaria. You know our work, and it must be clear to you that it's useless for you to deny the charges against you. It doesn't pay. Really, you must be sensible. Please, help us. We think highly of those who can speak German as well as you do, even if they are Jews."

That was the introduction. After that, the attack: "Who gave you the information you had about the Skoda Works?"

Lederer knew he must not say the name Cernik. "I can only repeat what is already on record."

"That's no good. You know more. Speak!" The Gestapo officer took a cowhide whip from the table.

"I do not know," Lederer repeated.

The officer reddened. He questioned, fluttered his whip, cursed, and then beat Lederer's head with the thick end of his cowhide.

Lederer stood motionless.

The officer, roused by the prisoner's silence, ordered the waiting guard, *"Erste Stufe!"* (The first grade!)

The guard bound Lederer's hands behind his back. He opened a small white door to a room similarly equipped: it was a torture room. A rope with a hook hung by a pulley from the ceiling. The guard lifted Lederer and hung him by his hands a few centimeters above the floor.

The officer typed something in the adjacent room. When he finished, he read Lederer what he had written.

"Will you sign it?" he asked.

Lederer did not answer. He had fainted.

When he came round they sat him on a chair, and the officer roared at him, "Sign!"

"I can't move my hands," replied Lederer.

"You dog, you won't sign? . . . *Zweite Stufe!*" (Second grade!)

The guard took Lederer to the door. The SS officer took his right hand, straightened his fingers, and put them in the doorjamb. Then he slowly shut the door. Lederer tried to pull his fingers free, but the tip of his forefinger was crushed.

Commissar Rhode, the head of the division, entered the room. The interrogating officer reported his results. Rhode ordered Lederer's bleeding be attended to. The tip of his forefinger was hanging by a thin thread of skin.

"Why don't you sign?" Rhode asked. "Who, in your opinion, is going to win the war?"

"I don't know," replied Lederer.

"Do you dare doubt our victory?" Rhode threw Lederer to the floor. Lederer got up slowly.

Rhode repeated in a threatening voice, "Who is going to win the war?"

"I don't know," said Lederer, and Rhode again threw him to the floor.

Lederer lay there, unable to get up. He saw the big feet spread apart above him, the red face, the gaping, slavering mouth, spouting, "We shall win, but if we perish, the whole world will perish with us!"

Lederer did not sign. He was sent to the Little Fortress in Theresienstadt, then to the ghetto, and then to Birkenau with the comment "RU" in his file.

The SS officer from the political department of the Gestapo called out Lederer's name. He led him through the camp and handed him over to Pestek.

Lederer soon recovered from his wounds. The fresh air did him good. His knees felt horribly weak, but he tried to walk straight, a few steps before Pestek. When he got to the bridge, he felt he could go no farther. He leaned against the railing and cooled his hot, swollen eyes with the palm of his hand. From here the Auschwitz empire of death, only 3 kilometers away, looked quite innocent. Straight rows of barracks as far as he could see. Red slate roofs of the crematoriums. The long shiny train passing through what looked like the gate of a factory. Columns of trucks covered with canvas. Barbed wire fences in geometric rows. To passengers gazing from passing trains it would seem to be a huge industrial plant, well laid out and efficiently organized. A plant that employed prisoners of war who lived in work camps behind the barbed wire fences.

When they walked down the slope of the viaduct, Pestek asked, "Well, what happened?"

"Just as you said, Herr Rottenfuehrer. They will call me again."

"It will be worse next time. You should think of how to disappear!"

Lederer looked at Pestek, surprised. He wondered what he should say. His experience with Germans was as bad as it could be, especially with those who wore the skull-and-bones insignia. Pestek could be trying to trap him. Just like another SS Rottenfuehrer named Schneider. Karel Krasa had been talking about Schneider only a few days ago, warning his comrades against him. It was a story similar to his own. Schneider had offered to help two Poles escape from Auschwitz. A partisan car was to wait for them next to the viaduct. The Poles paid well in advance. One morning, Schneider took the prisoners to the viaduct and returned to the camp. Everything seemed to be in order. The Poles who knew about it praised Schneider and said, "How good of him!" A week later two mutilated bodies were brought from the Auschwitz pit to the crematorium. Filip Mueller was in the process of cremating them, when he tore the shirt of one of them on a hook. On the chest of the body was scrawled: "Blockfuehrer Schneider betrayed us. Avenge our death!"

Schneider was handsome, smiling, blond. Lederer knew him. He used to bring the parcels that came by post to the family camp.

Pestek seemed to read what was in Lederer's mind. He moved closer to the prisoner. When he was quite near to him, he said, "Maybe you don't believe me because of this uniform. But you needn't be afraid. I am not a Nazi. Not one of them." And he began to talk about his youth in Bessarabia, his recruitment into the SS, how he was wounded near Stalingrad and then, after recovering and more training, was sent to Auschwitz to be a concentration camp guard.

To convince Lederer, Pestek said, "I do not want gold or money. What I do want is your promise that you will help hide me and another person whom I want to help."

"Who?" asked Lederer.

"You will learn when the time comes. I will come to see you in three days and then we will talk some more."

They were now near the big red brick building of the main guardhouse. A convoy of covered trucks approached from behind. When they arrived in the family camp Pestek handed Lederer over to Blockfuehrer Perschel.

Pestek had already thought out the plan for René's escape. He knew the prisoner who collected the bodies of the deceased every day and removed them from the camp on his cart. The identification and registration of the bodies was done by the SS guards on duty at the main gate of the camp. For a bottle of brandy, the prisoner would take out the "dead" body of René on the day Pestek was on duty at the gate. She would then be taken to an empty barracks on the way to the mortuary, where she would change into the uniform of an SS woman guard and wait for Pestek. From there they would go to the railway station and take a train to Krakow. Even if the Kapo of the *Leichenkommando* was not yet willing to cooperate, Pestek believed he could acquire another prisoner from Neumann's squad that collected corpses.

As a disabled soldier, Pestek was entitled to take a long leave. He had already applied for one, explaining that he wanted to visit his sick parents in Rumania. During his leave he would find a hiding place for René and himself, where they would stay until the war was over.

Spring was penetrating even the barbed wire fences. The heavy clouds of fog were disappearing. The mud was gradually drying off the roads and the wind smelled of earth. Between the blocks some thin grass was making its way toward the sun; and the sun, fair and just, was generously slanting its golden rays to the earth. Willy Brachmann organized the work squads. He tried to wake up the remaining population of the family camp from their deadly lethargy.

In block no. 7 the block woman was telling her clerk to make up a list of prisoners who were to go without food for slacking off at work.

René refused to do it. "Why do you punish these wretched women?" she asked. "What's the purpose of their working or improving anything? Why should they and for whom? They all know that nothing else is in store for us but to go up through the chimney!"

There was a knock at the door, and Pestek came in. The block woman left. Pestek glanced at René, and there was guilt in his look.

"I have been longing to see you terribly, my darling. I have a bad conscience. I did not dare come." He timidly drew near René to embrace her.

She did not seem to be aware of what he was talking about. She looked in his face as if she did not know him. Then she said with a mocking laugh, "The lord has come to his harem. He can pick and choose whomever he likes and can pay for."

She waved with her hand to show him the destitute women on the three-tiered bunks. She swallowed and continued: "The thin ones for a piece of bread. The better, for a rag. The functionaries for cigarettes. The block woman for a piece of salami and some scent. We haven't got a *chambre separée.* But if you pay well, the block woman will let you have this wooden cage, and the *Torwache* [guard of the gate] will watch so as to make it nice and private for you. You are an SS, so you can have the prettiest, according to your desire. For a nice smile. For a frank look in your deceitful eyes. You can do it brutally and savagely like Buntrock, or in a refined way like Mr. Schwarzhuber, or scientifically like Dr. Mengele."

René spoke and her eyes sparked hatefully. Her cheeks were burning. She looked very beautiful. Pestek tried to mollify her.

"René, you are doing me wrong. I am really fond of you, more than of anybody!"

"Oh, how romantic!" René mocked him. She had heard of his role in the Heydebreck affair. "A handsome murderer loves a condemned woman and will assist at her execution."

Pestek was desperate. He did not expect to be treated with such contempt and disgust. Nevertheless, the longer he looked at her the more he realized how much he loved her. He felt he could not live without her.

"What can I do to prove how I love you?" he asked desperately.

"Get rid of Buntrock!" she said disdainfully.

"That's impossible. But I will do more," Pestek replied abruptly.

"What are you going to do? Will you take revenge on Schwarzhuber?" asked René, thinking of the commandant's behavior, which had offended Pestek just as much as herself.

"I will save you. I will take you away from here. We'll wait together in safety until the war is over."

René looked at him distrustfully. "You are crazy. It is impossible even for a mouse to get out of here. And even if it were possible," she said resolutely, "I wouldn't go without Mother."

There was no doubt that she meant it. Pestek had not thought about her mother. She did not fit into the plan that he was about to discuss with René. This complicated things immensely. Pestek became nervous and embarrassed. Without saying good-bye, he left and went straight to Lederer's block. He found him talking to Zeimer. Pestek listened, and after a while he dismissed Zeimer politely.

"Well?" he asked.

Lederer had several suggestions to make. They could have a hiding place ready somewhere near Auschwitz. They could hide there when going to the Gestapo, then leave and go from Krakow to Bohemia by train. Or Lederer could dig a hole in the ground under the barbed wire fence, camouflage it, then at night sneak out to the neighboring camp. There he could count himself among the other prisoners lining up for work in the morning. Thus the number of prisoners would be correct, and nobody would be missing. Both Lederer and Pestek could then meet at their hiding place. Zeimer was fixing an escape with a Soviet prisoner of war from Odessa, Lederer told him. The Russian was Buntrock's orderly and often came to the camp.

"Miroslav has a civilian overcoat, a watch, a knife, and a compass," Lederer said.

"Have they anywhere to go? Who will hide them?" Pestek asked.

"The Soviet parachutists and the Polish partisans," Lederer replied.

"That might be good enough for your clerk or even for you. But I'm SS. The partisans would shoot me down mercilessly. It would be no good to explain . . ."

After a silence, Pestek said in a cross voice, "You talk too much."

"Miroslav is reliable, I guarantee it," Lederer protested.

"Nobody knows whether he'll succeed or what would break him. Neither of us. If you couldn't keep your mouth shut, I would have to get rid of you; in fact I would have no choice in the matter."

They were both silent for a while. But then Pestek held out his hand, gave Lederer a crushing hand clasp, and said, "Let's be friends. Let Viktor and Siegfried make an agreement—for life or death. We'll escape in uniforms. Here is a list of things we need. I'll get the cloth, the ration cards, the train tickets, and the pistol. You will be able to get the other things in the camp. I have noticed that you know how to 'organize.' "

Slowly Lederer grew less and less distrustful. He and Pestek could now sit and talk together like old friends. Pestek talked about his plan, and they both thought of all possible contingencies. Viktor took Lederer into his confidence and told him about his love for René. He confessed he would like to come back and fetch her and her mother, as soon as he could get the papers and find a safe hiding place in Bohemia. He had noticed personal cars driven by SS officers arriving from time to time in Birkenau. They came from Katowice and Krakow. The officers often came to get prisoners who were to be questioned; they took them away in their cars and nobody ever saw them again. That's what Pestek was planning to do.

"We'll escape from here safely, Siegfried. I will see to that. But you will have to show what you can do back in your own country."

Lederer considered his companion's words and deeds. Pestek's affection for René was the driving force behind his plans. The thought of her dying in a gas chamber had brought him to the other side. Lederer admired Pestek, but he wondered whether his zest and vigor would last. They would have to hide. They would have to struggle for life. Pestek would soon realize that the life of a fugitive is not as romantic as he thought. The escape and subsequent rescue of René and her mother would be no Wild West adventure. Maybe that's how Pestek looked at it. He, Lederer, had nothing to lose. He would go home to his own people. Pestek, on the other hand, was leaving what had become part of his life. He was going to be a fugitive just as much among the Germans as among the Czechs. Would he be able to hold out? Would he change his mind at the last minute?

Pestek's eyes were clear and truthful. He did not seem to worry or hesitate. He took his pistol from the table and put it back in its holster. Then he got up to leave. He turned at the door and said again, lifting his forefinger, "The first and last commandment: not a word to anybody!"

Pestek's plan for the rescue of René and her mother was based on his knowledge of the *Fahrbereitschaft* (transportation office), where he had worked for two months as a driver and as a clerk. It was common practice that when the political department of the Gestapo in Katowice phoned and requested a prisoner for interrogation, a personal car with a driver was put at the disposal of the SS officer who escorted the prisoner. Pestek knew the names of those who worked in the political department of the Gestapo. If he could manage to obtain official stationery with the stamp of the Gestapo, the rest would be easy.

The driver from the *Fahrbereitschaft* would take Lederer in an SS uniform to the gate of the Czech Family Camp. Pestek would phone Birkenau's camp office and, in the name of the Gestapo, request that René and her mother be brought to the main gate, to be taken for interrogation. Lederer would produce the appropriate papers with the stamp of the Gestapo and take charge of the two women. Pestek would be waiting along the road outside the camp. They would kill the driver and take the body to one of the deserted houses nearby. They would then drive some 50 kilometers to the railway station near the border. From there an express train would take them to Bohumin.

Chapter 13

The Password: Tintenfass

FROM THAT DAY ON Pestek often came to Lederer's block. Zeimer usually left without having to be told.

"Why is Pestek so interested in you?" Zeimer asked his friend.

"He has a girl in the camp and he wants to 'organize,' " Lederer said.

"I know the girl. It's René Karen, a blonde from number seven. She's worth it," Zeimer said.

Blockfuehrers from other parts of the camp used to come to the block as well. They looked for valuables. Whatever they found they just "confiscated" into their own pockets, shouting, threatening, and sometimes beating. They turned everything upside down, particularly in the block men huts. They searched all possible hiding places, tearing up the walls, the floor. But the bunk space was searched only at random. The "gentlemen" didn't like going there; they were discouraged by the placards hanging on the wall next to the entrance: *Eine Laus dein Tod* (A louse is your death).

Typhoid fever did not halt for an SS uniform. The block men relied on that fear. They hid their valuables in the bunks. The most valuable things and those that would be considered conspiracy-related were hidden in the pillows of the sick; none of the SS dared touch them. Nevertheless, it was a good block man's duty to be informed about everything in the block and to prevent any mishaps. He knew and observed his "organizers" and controlled the contraband without them knowing anything about it.

Zeimer once found the former owner of a fashionable Prague tailor's shop, whose name was Rosenbaum, fiddling with something on the top bunk. Zeimer climbed up and saw Rosenbaum sewing a military blouse.

"For whom?" he asked, frightened.

"For Rottenfuehrer Pestek," the tailor replied quietly.

Another time he surprised the shoemaker Rubinstein, who was polishing a military belt and making a leather holster for a pistol. Then he found in the pillow of Gregor the goldsmith a belt buckle with the inscription *Meine Ehre heisst Treue* (My honor is loyalty).

He put the buckle in his pocket so he could show it to Lederer. They called Gregor to the hut and showed him the buckle.

"For whom?"

Gregor glanced at Lederer and replied quietly, "For Rottenfuehrer Pestek."

From then on Zeimer did not worry anymore. If it's for our SS Blockfuehrer, he thought, there can be no harm in it, and it's all the better for the block.

Lederer struck one item after the other from his list. In the evening he would sneak out and carry the items to the empty washroom. There he hid them in a double wall. Each time he put a new item into place, he camouflaged it carefully with a pile of wood chips used to dry and sweep the concrete floor. It occurred to him that Zeimer's dark overcoat would be useful, too.

A month after the Heydebreck action, Pestek came riding into the camp on a bicycle. He didn't even stop at the guardhouse, but propped his bike against the wall of block no. 8, took his briefcase from the handles, and entered Lederer's hut. He took a pistol and a cap with the skull-and-bones emblem out of his briefcase. Lederer was stunned when he saw the cap.

Pestek noticed Lederer's reaction and said, "You'll have to get used to it; it's the best disguise you can have."

Then he taught Lederer how to use the pistol, whose chambers were empty.

"This is the end of stage one. The next stage will come in two days. When you see my bicycle standing next to the back wall of the washroom, near the concrete water tank, *then* you'll know that our day has come. That day I will bring you your braids. Have you a reliable watch?" he asked.

"Yes, a good Omega," replied Lederer.

Zeimer was out collecting the food supplies, so Lederer lifted the table board and removed a wooden stop from one of the legs of the table. Using a wire he maneuvered a piece of paper out of the opening. It was a report from the main camp, which included a plan of the Birkenau camps with the crematoriums marked in red.

During the last days of March, Lederer became nervous and surly even with Zeimer. He hated pretending to be interested in Zeimer's ever-changing plans of escape.

On April 5, after 6:00 P.M., when he was returning to the block, he saw Pestek's bicycle leaning against the far corner of the washroom. He already had his braids in his pocket and was ready to leave this damned part of the world forever. Two hours to go. The suffering that he had gone through with his comrades had strengthened his ties to them. He loved them even more than the outsiders he had known for years. He promised himself to do whatever he could to help save them.

Zeimer came back from the evening food rationing—a quarter of a piece of sawdustlike bread and a spoonful of beet-root jam. He sat down on the bunk and said, "Krasa and his friends haven't been to see us from the main camp for a long time."

"They are disturbed because Buntrock is supposed to have heard that the mechanics have warned us," explained Lederer.

"How do you know that?" asked Zeimer.

"Krasa's wife Elly, who deals with the parcels at our *Schreibstube* (office) got an urgent message from her husband. I'll know more tonight. In a little while, we shall meet at Dr. Milek's in the infection block. The moon is out. Could you lend me your overcoat so the guard won't spot me?"

"Gladly," said Zeimer. He went to the block and got his coat.

That day, as Rapportfuehrer Buntrock was taking over guard duty from Rottenfuehrer Perschel, the air in the block leaders' room was dense and full of smoke. There were cigarette butts everywhere on the floor and an empty bottle on the table. Pestek entered the room. They exchanged greetings and put a new bottle on the table. Buntrock smelled of liquor already; he looked at the label with an expert eye and read slowly, "*Wo-d-ka fy-po-ro-wa.*" Then he added, "The Poles are swine, but their liquor is excellent."

Perschel put glasses in front of each of them, and Pestek poured. They lifted their glasses and clinked them.

"A toast to your leave, Viktor!"

"To your Polish brunette sweetheart Zosza!" said Buntrock, lifting his glass.

"To a happy end of the war," said Pestek. They drank.

"Listen, Viktor," Buntrock babbled, "tell that sweetheart of yours that I'll come to see her up in Myslowice when I get my leave. Don't forget, or else I'll tell her all about that blonde from no. 7. She can come and have a go at her."

Buntrock could hardly stand on his feet. He looked at his watch.

"It's past seven. I have to get over to the barracks. Coming, Viktor?"

"The train leaves in an hour, and it's cold at the railway station. I'd rather wait here," Pestek said, excusing himself.

Buntrock said no more. He just staggered out of the door into the darkness.

The room was small, and the air was hot and stuffy. Perschel was half drunk. He opened his shirt at the neck, then took it off altogether and hung it on the peg. He returned to the table, sat down again, and started dozing. Soon he was snoring loudly. Pestek went to the peg and removed Perschel's military pay book from the breast pocket. He impatiently looked at his watch, smoking one cigarette after another. It was one minute to eight.

Meanwhile, Lederer was getting ready. He changed into an SS Untersturmfuehrer uniform in the darkness of the washroom. His Omega watch showed thirty seconds to eight. Lederer fixed the thick silver braids of a *Sonderdienst* on his shoulder. He propped Pestek's bicycle against the gate and hung the briefcase on the handles, but his eyes never left the narrow beams of light coming from the insufficiently blacked out guardroom window.

At the lower end of the camp, a red light appeared three times. An invisible hand moved it up and down. Lederer mounted the saddle of Pestek's bicycle; it was too high for him, and he could barely touch the pedals. He did not feel safe riding on the muddy and uneven road. He stopped in front of the gate, which was dimly lit by two bulbs fixed on concrete pillars.

"Halt. Who is there?" Pestek called out as he came out the door.

"Der Sonderdienst," replied Lederer, as they had agreed.

Pestek entered the guardroom, shook the groggy Perschel, and told him to open the gate for the *Sonderdienst*.

"It's eight o'clock. The train leaves in half an hour," Pestek said, fixing his belt and his pistol.

Rottenfuehrer Perschel adjusted his uniform, hurrying down the stairs and to the gate. He was happy that the *Sonderdienst* had not come in and seen the mess in the guardroom. He saluted, unlocked the gate and opened it, wished Pestek a nice journey, and returned to the guardroom.

Lederer walked the bicycle next to Pestek. They went to Auschwitz by the same route as they had the other day. Now it was lit by bulbs fixed on the pillars that supported the barbed wire fence. The lights of cars blinded them. Once they had to jump into a ditch to protect themselves. The wind made the canvas tops of the passing trucks flap open. They saw cowering women and children being driven to the crematoriums. A guard was in the watchtower at the end of the camp.

"Halt. Who goes there?" the guard shouted and threw light on the two men with the watchtower spotlight.

"Ah, Viktor, it's you," he said easily. "And who is that with you?"

"*Sonderdienst,*" replied Pestek. "He was held up back in our camp."

"Pass." The SS guard waved them on in a friendly way and switched off the lights.

They didn't turn right as Lederer expected, but proceeded straight, past the barracks and the SS hospital. Pestek put the bicycle in a stand in front of the dimly lit canteen, and walked to the road, which was even more brightly lit. Just before the crossroad, there was a gate and another guard tower right behind it.

"Halt! Who goes there?" a guard cried out as he climbed down the ladder. Viktor felt under his coat for the sharp dagger he had sewn into the lining. The guard came over and shone a light on their faces. His flashlight stopped on Lederer's silver braids.

"The password!" he demanded.

"*Tintenfass*" (the inkpot), they both answered in one breath.

"Pass," said the SS guard, and he lifted the gate.

It was twenty minutes past eight when they reached the railway bridge. A blacked-out train was coming into the Auschwitz station.

"That's our train!" cried Pestek. He caught Lederer's hand and they both rushed down the slope via a shortcut that led straight to the platform. The train had started moving when they jumped up onto the last car, opened the lock, and squeezed themselves in.

They were in the corridor, which was jammed with civilian passengers. The coach was dark and smelly. Their eyes slowly got accustomed to the darkness. In the light of a single blue bulb they could distinguish the faces of peasant women in scarves, workers in flat caps, and peasant men in fur caps. People slept leaning against the walls. Some lay in the corridor on their bundles, bags, and old suitcases. Some talked. Lederer and Pestek made their way through the heaps of luggage to the next car. But it was no better. The train was packed.

People stopped talking when they saw the SS uniforms. Suddenly, a gloomy mood settled over the car. The atmosphere grew tense, and there was hatred in the eyes that peered through the dark. In the next car the two fugitives found a place to sit. It was in an aisle next to the lavatory.

"We'll change in Cidice and take an express train to Bohumin and Prague," Pestek said triumphantly, as if this were the end of their dangerous journey.

"But how will we cross the frontier? I have no documents," Lederer reminded him.

Pestek took Perschel's stolen pay book out of his pocket.

"For the time being you will have to make do with this."

"But the papers will be closely examined at the frontier," Lederer said, looking at Perschel's card. "Will this be good enough?"

The local train reached the frontier in an hour's time. Cidice. Lederer's apprehensions were to be proved correct. They did not get out of the train, but looked out of the window, watching the bustle. Military police in green uniforms were strolling on the platform. They had brass plates hanging from their necks with the inscription *Feldpolizei*.

They stopped soldiers, officers, and civilians and examined their papers thoroughly. Pestek was unnerved. He had not considered the possibility of military police. He stayed with Lederer in the empty car to ponder the situation. Lederer suggested that they get out and walk over the frontier.

"Do you know the country around here?" asked Pestek.

"I only know the road to Bohumin," Lederer answered.

"Then it will be safer to go by train. We'll wait in the car until the express train arrives," decided Pestek. They leaned out of the window and saw some customs officers joining the police. The platform was now empty; the officials were waiting for the next train.

Soon an international express train came rattling into the station. Pestek saw what he was looking for: the mail van was the next-to-last car.

"Come on, it's time," he said to Lederer, pulling him out. They ran to the end of the express train. The police did not notice them; they were too busy looking through the papers of passengers who had just arrived. Two SS officers in black boots and carrying briefcases nimbly climbed onto the train and disappeared into the mail van while the dispatcher signaled the express off.

"*Heil Hitler! Paketenkontrolle*" (examination of parcels), Pestek said in a sharp, commanding voice, lifting his right hand. There were two attendants in creased navy blue uniforms. They stepped back without a word of protest or enquiry, leaving the uninvited visitors to do whatever they wanted.

The mail van was half filled with parcels, suitcases, and boxes. The pretenders sorted out the goods and put aside "suspicious" parcels. They opened some of them, and when they found nothing suspicious, they ordered, "Pack it up again!"

"Nasty Germans!" one of the railwaymen said in Czech. "They rob even the poor people who get parcels from their relatives laboring in the Reich."

Lederer was affected by this unflattering remark, though it was addressed to Pestek, who was cutting off some bread and salami. Pestek even put a few boxes of sardines in his pockets, pretending indignation at a "treasonous" letter found at the bottom of a box of soap powder. A Czech worker who had been taken to the Reich had written to his friend, telling him the truth about his toil and drudgery, and warning him about going to the Reich.

The railwaymen were surprised to see these officers checking the mail, but they thought it would be unwise to argue or to call the engineer. The two SS officers wrote down the date of a few parcels, put them aside, and declared them "confiscated." Then they left, looking confident, and found an empty car. When the train passed Ostrava, they moved to the dining car. Breakfast was served when the train reached Olomouc. According to the clock on the platform, it was 7:00 A.M.

At the same time, in Birkenau, the prisoners in the family camp were lining up for the morning roll call. The block men shouted nervously, urged the prisoners to stand in straight lines and counted them. One person was missing. They ran to Lageraelteste Brachmann, who sent them back to count again and to search in the blocks.

Willy had already been informed about Lederer's disappearance. Zeimer had discovered it soon after midnight. When he noticed that Lederer had not returned from the "secret meeting," he dressed and went to the infection block. He persuaded the prisoner who guarded the entrance to let him see Dr. Milek.

"Lederer was never here," said the physician, half asleep.

Zeimer now understood the connection between the shirt, the buckle, and the overcoat. He wanted Siegfried to get as big a head start as possible, so he didn't report his absence until the morning.

Rapportfuehrer Buntrock arrived in the camp. His huge body strode to the wooden counter next to the office. Willy Brachmann, in a well-tailored, striped prisoner's uniform, rushed to him from the head of the prisoners' formations. He ran like a horse that had been well trained; he stopped at the correct distance, removed his cap, dropped his arms, and reported, "There are 4,063 Jewish prisoners in custody of the B-II-b division of the camp lined up to the morning roll call. Prisoner no. 170521 is missing."

"Who is it?" Buntrock asked, irritated.

"Blockaelteste Siegfried Israel Lederer."

Buntrock's face grew red and the veins on his temples pulsed with blood. He struck Willy in the face with his whip and roared, "You dog, why didn't you report it earlier? All prisoners will stand here until the Jewish dog is brought back!"

Ten minutes after Buntrock's departure, all hell broke loose. The sirens announced the escape of a prisoner throughout the Auschwitz complex. Kapos with sticks poured out of the main camp. From the SS barracks, armed SS on motorcycles sped out. Another group of SS, with their barking, snapping bloodhounds, rushed into the family camp. The dogs sniffed at the fugitive's bunk and then ran out of the camp toward the SS barracks. A Gestapo car from Auschwitz came to get Brachmann and Zeimer.

While the train with the fugitives was drawing near Prague, the Auschwitz Gestapo was sending out a cable. The teleprinter brought the cable to Adolf Eichmann's office in the *Reichssicherheitshauptamt* in Berlin; to Pohl's Inspectorate of Concentration Camps in Oranienburg; to the Petchek house of the Prague Gestapo; to all district commanders; and to Stapo (state police), Kripo (criminal police), and Greko (frontier guards) officers. It read:

JEWISH PRISONER IN PROTECTIVE CUSTODY LEDERER SIEGFRIED BORN 6.3.1904 IN ALBER DISTRICT TACHOV ESCAPED AT NIGHT 5 APRIL 1944 FROM THE CONCENTRATION CAMP AUSCHWITZ II STOP ALL INVESTIGATIONS SO FAR UNSUCCESSFUL STOP START SEARCHING INDEPENDENTLY STOP THE SS REICHSFUEHRER ALREADY INFORMED . . .

Pestek was officially on leave, and his name was not yet connected with Lederer's.

The express train reached the main station in Prague at noon. Lederer and Pestek carefully watched the platform before getting off the train. They saw no uniforms with the *Feldpolizei* insignia. Pestek and Lederer entered the restaurant from the platform and took seats where they could keep an eye on both exits. They discussed what they had to purchase. They had some money, two diamonds, and a golden bracelet.

First they looked for a secondhand dealer. Lederer sold the bracelet for a tidy sum of money. Then he bought a well-made secondhand green suit, shoes, linen, a cap, and tie. Pestek chose a good secondhand gray coat, similar to what Lederer had borrowed from Zeimer. Then they went to the public baths. After taking time to rest, Lederer changed into his civilian clothes and Pestek put a civilian coat over his uniform. They also detached the skull-and-bones from their caps. In the afternoon they bought badges with swastikas and two Iron Crosses in the form of a pin. The dealer sold them the Nazi emblems only when Pestek produced his papers proving his right to wear them.

They had their supper in a small pub near the old "Little Quarter" square. The room was packed with soldiers from the army as well as from the SS who came to spend their leave or passed through Prague on their way home or to the front. Pestek talked with them and made enquiries about the examination of papers and billeting in barracks or other military dormitories. Soon he knew all he needed to know. Many soldiers were drunk. Pestek was tempted to try and steal some more papers, as he had done in Birkenau. But after his fifth glass of beer he became tired. He could not keep his eyes open and did not want to hear or do anything.

Lederer urged him to leave.

"Where are we going for the night?" Pestek asked.

"We'll have to try to sleep in the train tonight, but we'll have a good bath and a bed tomorrow. I promise."

They went to the Smichov railway station and left for Plzen shortly before midnight.

Chapter 14

In Plzen

THE CABLE announcing Lederer's escape had been received by Prague Gestapo Commissar Horat Stiewitz. Stiewitz had come to Prague from Munich as an experienced criminologist. He was an old member of the Nazi party and bore a scar on his forehead from his part in suppressing the workers' strikes in the Ruhr as an SA stormtrooper.

For Stiewitz, this case came as no surprise. He remembered Lederer as a pigheaded man and a member of the Weidman group. Now he went through his record again and ordered instructions to be sent out. He had Lederer's photograph brought from the archives, copied, and sent with a warrant to all Gestapo offices, to Czech and German police stations, and to all frontier guard commanders.

Stiewitz also sent a special message to the Plzen Gestapo commander. In Plzen, a list was made of all persons under suspicion of ever having known or been in touch with Lederer. The Plzen Gestapo official entrusted with the case studied the list and marked with a cross all names whose homes were to be occupied and watched and, with a circle, names of suspicious persons to be followed. The Nazi machinery was at work.

Lederer had reckoned with the Nazi tactics. He was no novice. He knew a little about criminology, and he had experienced the Gestapo methods firsthand. In the train he thought of all possible names connected with him. Had it been possible to compare the Gestapo chief's list with that in Lederer's mind, many of the names would have been identical. He had to avoid these friends at all cost. He knew they would be watched. But he was relying most on Cernik the tailor to help him and on Gitta Steiner, who now had Aryan papers and lived under the name Skala. The Gestapo apparently knew nothing about her, he realized when he was questioned in Auschwitz. Nor could the Gestapo know about one of his relatives in Plzen; he had never mentioned him to anybody. But Lederer was not sure he would be able to find him at his old address on Sedlackova Street.

The water was boiling on a gas cooker. Kveta Sindelar was preparing her husband's breakfast in her small, old-fashioned kitchen. She put some ersatz coffee into the pot and was just pouring the milk into another pot when the bell rang. Mrs. Sindelar went to the hall to open the door. She hesitated for a moment. It was early, and it was wartime. She could not think of anybody who would be calling on them. She heard somebody knock timidly.

"Who is it?" she asked.

"It's me, Siegfried!"

Mrs. Sindelar did not recognize the voice, but she unlocked the door. Two men entered the dim little hall. The shorter of the two took off his cap and held his hand out to her. His face seemed faintly familiar. But the other one, standing there in a military uniform and in black boots, frightened her.

Siegfried! She hadn't seen him for a long time. She was told he'd been taken by the Gestapo. Now he looked older, his face strained, but his hair was as black and curly as ever. The blue eyes, the nose, yet—yes, it was Siegfried, her husband's cousin!

But what about the soldier, with his black lapels and the silver thunderbolts on his sleeves? What had Siegfried to do with him?

She took them into the kitchen, hesitating a little. Then she went to wake up her husband. They all sat down at the kitchen table and had some coffee and gingerbread. Lederer told them he had proved to be a good worker in the camp. Now he had been sent as a specialist to do some assembly work in a new work camp in the Reich. This soldier was escorting him. "He's a nice guy," Lederer went on. "I persuaded him to interrupt our journey in Plzen, and I told him he might get accommodations for a day or two." The couple looked embarrassed.

They had little room for themselves in the apartment, and now two more people? Lederer would not back down. He talked about what he had suffered from the Gestapo and what it was like in Germany. The Nazis' days are numbered, and the end of the war is imminent, he said. The soldier who accompanied him was not really a German; he had come from Rumania and had saved his life.

Pestek looked uneasy, but when Lederer whispered something in his ear, he knew immediately what to do. He took some cigarettes out of his pocket and offered them to Mr. Sindelar. Then he put some more cigarettes and cigars on the table. Mr. Sindelar smoked contentedly, but from time to time he interrupted Lederer's prattling with a question. He scrutinized Pestek's face.

When they had finished their coffee, he got up and said, "I must be off. Naturally you may stay, Siegfried, and the soldier can stay with you and have a rest as well, since he has been as good as you say. It's forbidden, but all the same, he seems to deserve it, doesn't he?"

Mrs. Sindelar, who had been reluctant earlier, became very friendly. She brought some jam, bread, and salami. But her guests were too tired to eat. They forgot about their plans, about René and Auschwitz. Everything was now meaningless. They only wanted to rest.

"Kveta, we've been traveling for two days. We can't go on. We must have some sleep," said Lederer.

Mrs. Sindelar brought the feather beds. For the soldier she made a bed in the lumber room and for Siegfried a couch in the bedroom.

When Lederer woke up, it was nearly twelve o'clock. At first he did not know where he was, but then he heard Pestek snoring in the next room. That reminded him of their precarious situation. They were pressed for time. He quickly left his warm bed, put on his trousers and boots, and as he buttoned his shirt, went to the kitchen. Mrs. Sindelar had laid the table and was warming up the soup. Siegfried quickly shaved and washed. Then he ate and answered Kveta's questions as best as he could. He felt awkward and ashamed. He did not like deceiving her, but there was no other way.

He went back to the lumber room and looked at Pestek, who was sleeping like a baby. Lederer put the military blouse over his pullover and took his overcoat. Then he went to the kitchen and said, "I am going to see some friends, Kveta. I may even stay overnight. Tell Viktor to stay and wait for me here and give him this little note, will you?"

The staircase of the house was dark. Lederer got the holster and the pistol out of his briefcase and set the military cap on his head in a rakish manner.

He was back home again. He had not seen Plzen for five years, but the town looked the same, as if nothing had happened during his absence. It was the time of day when the morning shift ended. People were hurrying home. Some young men joined the girls who were strolling in the streets. Lederer saw pretty young mothers pushing wicker carriages, letting their babies enjoy the warmth of the first spring sunlight. The bells of the red streetcars tinkled, and white chestnut blossoms lined the paths in the park. The streets were bordered with blooming pansies. Trucks carrying beer barrels labeled *Prazdroj* were leaving the gates of the city brewery. Only the smoke coming from the chimneys of the Skoda Works reminded Lederer of other pretty young mothers who were at this very moment entering gas chambers where they would become little particles of ashes and smoke scattered in the universe.

Some large red posters drew Lederer's attention. A long list of names in black. Sentenced to death. Executed. Shot. Whole families with children. The offense: providing shelter for persons who were not registered with the police, to partisans, agents, or prisoners. He was stunned. His good-natured cousin could have no idea of the risk he was taking.

Lederer had to know whether the Gestapo was searching for him already. There was a house near the railway station where he used to live before the war. Lederer decided to go there and look up his neighbor Eda Kotora. A big poster on the railway station read: *Fuehrer befiehl, wir folgen* (Fuehrer commands, and we obey).

Lederer found the street he was looking for and walked along the left side of the road. On the other side he saw a man wandering about, wearing glasses and a gray overcoat.

Lederer decided instead to go to see Pachman, his old schoolmate. Pachman used to be a very good student. He played chess and was good at sports. He never cared about politics, but was ready to help. Lederer had left him his camera, family heirlooms, and some papers just before he was taken. He could use them now. Should he risk it? Pachman's name had never been mentioned by the police or by the Gestapo. Lederer found Taborska Street and the house. He knew it well. He looked around to see if he had been followed and then went up to the first floor. The name Jaroslav Pachman was on a small plaque on a door. A young woman opened it when he knocked. She was nice-looking and had large, vivid eyes.

"What can I do for you?" she asked in German when she saw the military cap and the boots.

Lederer was confused. Was this the right address? He asked in Czech, "Is this the flat of Jaroslav Pachman?"

"Yes," she answered in Czech. "What do you want from him?"

"He used to be my schoolmate and a good friend of mine. I am passing through to my formation and haven't seen him for years."

"Come at three o'clock. He should be back from work by then," Pachman's wife replied. She started to close the door.

"I am sorry to trouble you," Lederer insisted, "but I am tired and pressed for time. I'd rather wait here, if you don't mind."

He entered. The room was nice and cozy. The young woman waved him to an armchair, politely but coldly. Then she excused herself and left. A baby was playing in the next room. After about ten minutes, he heard the key turn in the front door. A tall, blond man came in and was surprised at the sight of the man in the uniform.

"Don't you recognize me? I am Siegfried!" Lederer got up and put out his hand.

Pachman paled. He clasped Lederer's hand and said, "My God, you must leave quickly. The Gestapo is after you. I had a message this morning from mutual friends. It's quite possible that the Gestapo followed you. You must realize that I have a wife and a child to look after."

Pachman brought Lederer's Leica camera and a small case containing his family treasures.

"Is it true that you have escaped from a concentration camp?" he asked. "And in this disguise?"

Lederer rolled up his sleeve. Pachman saw the tattooed number on his left arm. He did not know what to do. He wanted to help Lederer. He was very fond of him.

"You must understand, Siegfried. I would love to do more for you, but we have a baby." He was almost begging. His voice quavered.

Lederer thanked him and accepted the few bank notes that Pachman forced on him. When he was leaving, Pachman said, "Please, Siegfried, not a word to anybody. It would be the end of us all."

"You can count on it. I haven't been here. Good-bye, and thanks!"

Lederer looked out cautiously from the staircase window. There was nothing in the street that aroused his suspicion, so he left the house. Then he looked for a call box. He wanted to get in touch with Rudolf Steiner's daughter. He did not know her personally, but he did know that she was young, energetic, and a brunette. He also knew that she had Aryan papers from her relatives and that she was working as a typist and interpreter at the Skoda Works in Plzen. That was all he remembered from what Steiner had told him.

He went to a call box, dialed the number, and asked for Miss Gitta

Skala. After a while, he heard her ask in German, "What can I do for you?"

Lederer replied in German as well. He introduced himself as Captain Hans Gronke and said, "I am passing through to the front and have a message for you from Rudolf. He was wounded when transported."

Gitta replied, "You can come and see me tomorrow. I live at 46 Sadova."

Lederer felt it was dangerous for Pestek and him to stay in Plzen and that they should disappear as soon as possible. He was relying on Gitta to provide them with papers and money. But the most important thing of all was a hiding place, a *reliable* hiding place. And that could be secured only by somebody who knew the network of members of Colonel Weidman's resistance group.

A group of women and children, deceived by SS men into waiting for baths and disinfection, have no idea that they await their death in the gas chambers. SS photo, June 1944.

Deported Jews ordered for selection at Birkenau platform by SS selection staff. In the background, the entrance gate to Birkenau. At left, barracks of women's camps section B-I-a.

Part of the quarantine camp B-II-a. Photo taken in 1946.

Inside a wooden barrack in the Czech Family Camp

Of the five Birkenau camps of section B-II, only the former quarantine camp B-II-a was preserved as part of the Polish State Museum.

The pond near the crematorium where the ashes of the dead were poured out.

The ruins of the Birkenau camp. At present, part of the Polish State Museum in Auschwitz-Birkenau.

What remains today of the barracks of camp section B-II. Still standing are chimneys from the heating channels.

Chapter 15

A Hiding Place

JOSEF CERNIK LIVED with his wife, Antonie, in Doubravka, in the suburbs of Plzen. Years ago he had worked in the mines of Kladno, but had been fired because he took part in a strike. After that he took up his former profession, that of tailor. He moved to Plzen, and after a while he and his wife built a little house and set up a tailor shop in the basement. But they did not do very well for themselves. His wife helped in the business, but she reproached her husband because he spent so much time on his political activities that he had little energy left for his work. He got in touch with many people and tried to learn whether they would be reliable. He sewed for them, even if they couldn't afford to pay him. He advised and helped when they were in danger and, most important, he knew of places where people could hide.

He had helped the Weidman group before Lederer was taken. He was questioned and beaten, but he did not talk. He said only that he had made a suit for Lederer. Cernik liked Lederer. He had maintained contact with him when he was in Theresienstadt through Vesely the barber. Lederer had last sent him a message about six months ago, a little before he was transported to Auschwitz.

Lederer knew there were two possibilities: Cernik could either be in prison or at home. If at home, he would be watched by the Gestapo. He lived about an hour's walk from the center of town. Lederer knew the house. He had called there several times. He went to the bus stop and took a bus marked "Doubravka." He got out at the next-to-last stop and turned on to a path leading to some woods. There he found a spot hidden behind a hawthorn shrub from which he could observe Cernik's house. He saw the upper and lower windows as well as the door of the house from a distance of about 100 meters. He could also watch the dirt path that led across the meadows from the bus stop to the scattered little houses.

Lederer settled comfortably amid the shelter of the shrubs. He got out some food and opened a box of sardines with his knife. It was the box that Pestek had taken in the mail van. It was a nice day, and the sun was warm; only toward evening did it get colder. Lederer waited half an hour, then an hour. Time seemed to pass more and more slowly, and Lederer was beginning to get nervous. The house seemed empty. Was Cernik really in prison? What could they do? Where would they sleep? Where could they hide? Where would they get their food? They might be able to make do and sleep in haystacks, in huts, under bridges, in the woods, in deserted chalets—that could be done for a week or two. But what then? He looked at his watch again. It was half past six. He had been waiting for two hours. He looked toward the bus stop. A bus had just arrived, and people were getting out of it. One of them approached Cernik's house. He was a tallish man in a leather coat and a brown hat. He walked confidently and without hesitation and entered the house without knocking. "A new owner of the house," Lederer said to himself, disappointed. He was going to pack and go. He broke his bread into the box of sardines to sop up the oil. He did not finish it. Suddenly he saw a small man in a gray coat and hat quickly leaving Cernik's house. "Cernik!" Lederer was ecstatic. But then he saw the little man carefully look around and immediately realized what was happening.

The house was being watched from the inside. He looked at the house again. A thin strip of light could be seen from the basement window, which was half hidden below the pavement.

Cernik went down the narrow wobbling stairs into his basement workshop. Cursing, he covered the window with a thin blanket. The Gestapo had been occupying his little house for two days now. A red-haired German had just arrived to replace a Czech plainclothes policeman.

Cernik took an unfinished jacket, lifted a trap door in the ceiling, and went up a few narrow steps to the room above. There a Gestapo officer was comfortably settled in a wicker armchair. He was reading a newspaper and drinking coffee. He had brought his own coffee, but Mrs. Cernik had to make it for him. She did not like doing it, but she preferred doing that to letting him go into the kitchen. She never liked the Germans, but ever since she had lost her relatives in Lidice she hated them. They did not even allow her to go and see the graves of the executed men. Neither did she receive letters from the cousin who was taken away to Germany with her little girl.

"I am going next door to try on this jacket," Cernik said to his wife and translated it into German, gnashing his teeth. Then he shut the door and listened to see whether he had been followed. He went around the house, trying to see in the darkness. Was it a military cap that he thought he saw somewhere around the corner? He quickly stepped back, intending to return home and inform the man inside. But somebody was softly drawing nearer, now without the cap on his head. Cernik immediately knew Lederer. Without uttering a word, they went to a small shed in the yard. After a while the tailor returned home.

"Vit wasn't in, so I have to finish the jacket without the fitting," he said, wiping his shoes on the mat. The German lifted his eyes and watched Cernik for awhile, then he went on reading his paper. Cernik went down to his workshop. There he opened the oblong window, and Lederer dropped onto the floor of the basement as softly as a cat.

"Quiet. The Gestapo officer is right above," Cernik told him with a finger on his mouth. "Go back, and after you pass the third house on your right, turn to your left. You will see a small bungalow where my brother-in-law lives. Tell him I sent you and wait for me there."

Lederer didn't wait long. Cernik came ten minutes later, and, after introducing Lederer to his brother-in-law, he took them to the back room and made some coffee. Lederer told them the story of his escape, as well as what was going on in Auschwitz.

"The beasts!" Cernik burst out when Lederer had finished his story.

"You must disappear from Plzen tomorrow with your Rumanian friend. That's clear." He thought for a little while, and then went on, "Do you know an inn called Ahoj in Zbraslav, next to the harbor?"

Lederer nodded, and Cernik continued, "It belongs to a man whose name is Mican. He is all right. You go there and ask for a beer. Then you just tell him quietly, 'I have word for you to come and fetch your suit from your tailor in Prague!' He will reply, 'My tailor doesn't live in Prague.' Then you will say, 'I've made a mistake, it's in Plzen.' And when he says, 'How is he getting on?' everything is in order. You can speak with him just as you speak with me. Mican will hide you well. Not even the devil will be able to find you."

It was getting late. At about ten o'clock Cernik switched off the light by turning the bulb in its socket. Lederer sneaked out the window and disappeared into the night.

The next day, at six o'clock in the evening, Lederer knocked at the door of Gitta Skala's flat. Pestek accompanied him. A brunette, about twenty-five years old, dressed fashionably, looked inquiringly at Lederer. She said, trying to look calm, "I was expecting you to come in uniform, and alone, Captain."

Lederer introduced himself. He said his own name and mumbled Pestek's name as well. He asked her to let them talk to her.

Gitta took them in, not without hesitation. The room was warm, furnished with taste. She knew the uniforms and ranks and was afraid of being trapped by the Gestapo.

"I am sorry I could not explain everything over the telephone. I would have preferred not surprising you," Lederer apologized as soon as they entered the room. And he explained why he was there. Gitta pressed Lederer to tell her about her father, and he did not conceal anything.

"His last breath, his last thought was of you," Lederer finished in German, so Pestek could understand.

The conversation hit a dead end, since Gitta was too distressed by the news of her father's death to continue talking.

"I can understand what this means to you. I am terribly sorry not to be able to console you. But believe me, I just can't. It's terrible to see somebody die in front of you, but to see thousands and tens of thousands of people die, as is happening in Auschwitz—that's impossible even to grasp. A human being just can't feel it or think about it. Something like that can only register when expressed in merciless, dry statistics. What is happening in Auschwitz today and every day and has been happening for years and is going on even now, this very minute, while we are having coffee in this lovely flat of yours. It is a crime so huge and monstrous that it's beyond any human conception or comprehension."

Lederer discussed with Gitta how to send a message abroad and how to warn the people in Theresiens adt. She listened attentively and was sympathetic when she heard from Pestek about René.

"What do you need most?" she asked.

"We need a lot. Identity cards, papers, money, and shelter," Lederer said.

"I can't provide all that at once, but I will try and get as much as I can," the young woman promised, touching her wavy hair.

Gitta was in contact with an engineer by the name of Faltys. At the beginning of the German occupation her father had saved him from the clutches of the Gestapo. Faltys could provide faultless Aryan papers. Many refugees had escaped the country with the false papers that he had provided them. His seals were made so well that they deceived even the SS from Eichmann's Emigration Center in Prague. Faltys was shrewd and careful. Gitta did not even know his address. They would meet at a different place each time. Nevertheless, she could reach him quickly enough through a third person. Gitta decided that she ought to introduce Lederer to Faltys personally.

"I will introduce you to a reliable man in Prague. He will be able to supply the papers for you. I'll come to Prague, and we shall all meet together. You can discuss everything with him in my presence, if you wish."

She fixed the time of the meeting. "You must be there on time. I would not be able to come again."

Then she brought out a thick envelope and gave it to Lederer. It contained bank notes, ration cards, and coupons. She explained in Czech, "You will find an identity card in it. It belonged to an engineer named Welker. He died in Dachau about a year ago. All you have to do is change the photograph."

Chapter 16

The Weekend House at Zbraslav

THE NEXT DAY the fugitives prepared for their journey. Kveta prepared a good breakfast. For three days they had felt comfortable and at home with the Sindelars. Kveta was sorry that Siegfried had to go. He consoled her. It would all be over soon, he promised. He would come to see them immediately after the war. Meanwhile, they could look for a wife for him. He kissed her good-bye and fastened a locket with a golden chain on her neck. It was one of the treasures he had inherited from his mother and had hidden with Pachman. Pestek gave Mr. Sindelar a box of cigars. Sindelar insisted on seeing them off.

Lederer and Pestek reached Zbraslav shortly after twelve o'clock. Lederer found the inn next to the harbor. Pestek had to wait outside so as not to arouse suspicion. Lederer wore civilian clothes, boots, and his overcoat. He took his coat off, found an unoccupied table, and sat down. He ordered presswurst with onions and scrutinized the innkeeper when he came to cut his coupons. When he saw him standing alone at the bar he went over, ordered a glass of beer, and started reciting the magic cant that Cernik had taught him. He had repeated it to himself in the train several times. Now the miracle happened. The innkeeper, a sturdy man of fifty, with a thick mane of blond hair and an energetic, oblong face, said at once, "I have no papers, but you can have a good, safe weekend cabin right now."

Lederer was overwhelmed. He told the innkeeper about Cernik, about the escape, and, then, at what he thought the right moment, about Pestek. The innkeeper knitted his brows in a deep frown. Siegfried had to explain at length before he dispelled Mican's distrust, especially when he heard about Pestek being SS. Mican took Pestek into the kitchen and there he questioned him. When they both returned to Lederer's table, Mican appeared to be satisfied. The Rumanian boy with the moustache seemed to have gained his confidence.

In the afternoon there were no guests in the inn. Mican sat down at the table and explained, "Our local Nazis have their special room at the back of the house. They call it the 'casino.' You should join them one day and see what information you can get from them. They won't talk in front of me, they know only too well how much I love them."

Then he instructed them about the weekend house: what they should and should not do, where they could get their water and their milk, how to open and close the door without a key, who came to the neighboring house, that they would have to disappear on weekends, and a lot of other useful advice. Then he took them to the empty casino and showed them a high, steep hill from the back window. Beyond the hill they saw the woods.

Mican explained, "You'll go through the woods until you come to a dirt road that will lead you into a little valley. There you'll see three weekend houses. The one with the yellow window shutters on the slope closest to the woods is yours. It belongs to Ada Kroupa from Prague. He spends Saturdays and Sundays in the cabin, so then you can sleep at Adolf Kopriva's villa, on the other side of the river."

Pestek and Lederer climbed up the hill and went through the low, fir-tree wood. In half an hour's time, a valley, glowing in the sunshine, lay before them. They immediately saw their cabin, with its yellow shutters, next to a group of firs. They rollicked like little boys and raced to the house. The door opened, according to the innkeeper's instructions, by a special turn of the knob. There was just one room with two beds, one on top of the other, mattresses, and two blankets. "Your hut in Auschwitz was no better," Pestek teased the former block man.

They opened the shutters and were overjoyed when they saw the view and all the luxuries in the little wooden cabin: a washbasin, a jug full of water, a little brick stove, shelves, wooden hangers. They lifted a square trap door in the floor and found a ladder leading underground. There was some sugar, kerosene, tea, a samovar, candles, and matches.

They undressed, took off their dusty shoes, washed at the brook, and lay down to have a good rest. The little log house had become their home for the night. They were fugitives no more.

The sun was already high when the shutters were finally opened and the two men, dressed only in their pants, made their way to the well. They had an appointment in Prague in a few days, but now they were happy to have a vacation. They spent their time mending and repairing their things and planning what to do next. First they needed papers. Even Pestek's papers were valid only for the trip to his parents in Rumania. They also needed some equipment. That could be obtained quite easily in Prague.

Prague was not far. They discussed who should go, and, for the first time, they could not agree. Pestek was frustrated. He was uneasy because all around him people spoke Czech and he could not understand them. He suddenly was afraid that Lederer would get rid of him now that he didn't need him anymore. He wanted to prove that he was useful. He didn't want to become a burden to his partner. Now he saw his opportunity. He would be all right in Prague, among the German soldiers. They argued who should go and who should stay, and suddenly Pestek burst out, "You are a prisoner, but keep running here and there and everywhere, and I, who should be your guard, must sit back and wait."

Lederer felt that it would be wise for him to yield. Pestek went to Prague in the afternoon. He had money enough to join some noisy soldiers he had met on the platform. They were passing through Prague on leave or on their way to the front. They wanted to enjoy themselves. Pestek drank with them, shouted, boasted, and talked like a soldier who had been at the front. He produced his Iron Cross and talked of his fighting on the Russian front. He showed them the wide scar on his left hip, and they showed their respect.

The exhilarated soldiers left their drink and girls and came to listen to what he had to say. Viktor stayed with them all night. As they changed pubs, wine, and beer, Pestek, unnoticed, secretly searched their overcoats and shirts and took as much as he could from their pockets. He especially looked for two pay books and leaves of absence. He toyed with a pistol that had been put aside. He felt safe; the military police did not bother these soldiers. They were not to be irritated or discouraged before their departure. They were to fight well and be full of enthusiasm for the Fuehrer's cause.

Late the following morning, Lederer was still asleep when the door of the cabin suddenly burst open. An army knapsack fell heavily onto the lower berth. Pestek started unpacking it, and Lederer was shocked to see what Pestek had brought: tins of food, cigarettes, underwear, a pistol, several rounds of ammunition, and grenades. Pestek weighed and turned them in his hands, stroked them. He remembered his first training camp in Poland, where he had been trained to fight in cities.

"Such grenades can cause a lot of commotion. You can dispose of a lot of people and be far off before anyone has time to recover," Pestek explained, handing one of them to Lederer.

He produced a mass of papers from his breast pocket. There was a new pay book, a leave of absence, and a travel order to the front. Pestek was very proud of his booty. His eyes glittered when he recounted his mischief. He showed Lederer how he had taken the things from his fellow SS soldiers, as well as from the Wehrmacht.

In the afternoon, they worked on the papers. Lederer exchanged the photograph of the deceased Welker for his own. He had found a snapshot in the family album at the Sindelars in Plzen. With india ink and other tools Pestek bought in Prague, Lederer completed the missing part of the stamp and fixed papers for Pestek. Viktor washed the linen, repaired their shoes, and cleaned the uniforms. They affixed new facings and officers' insignia. Lederer, who was older than Pestek, advanced to an Obersturmfuehrer. Pestek became an Untersturmfuehrer.

Then they discussed how they could get the money they needed. They would need a lot to support four persons. Lederer estimated what he could get for his Leica. He reverently looked at his mother's jewels.

"I had lots of such things in Auschwitz," Pestek said.

"Stolen things won't bring you luck," Lederer replied.

"All we have is stolen. Stolen things have saved us, kept us alive, and helped us to pull through. Do you think I should have just sat idly by as the others—prisoners, Blockfuehrers, and officers alike—stuffed their pockets full of things that belonged to the deportees? Why should I? I wasn't as stupid as that, and, besides, I have . . . "

He did not finish the sentence. He remembered René and that prevented him from telling Lederer about his mistress, Zosza. He was ashamed to say that he had a lover in Myslowice. He used to escape from the nightmare of Auschwitz's chimneys into the arms of that brunette. He had met her in a nightclub in Krakow soon after his arrival in Poland. Zosza had invited him to her shabby little flat in Myslowice. Viktor had rewarded her munificently. From then on he used to visit her regularly, bringing all sorts of jewels and valuables from the camps like a magpie to his nest: precious diamonds, brooches, pearls, necklaces. Zosza was thrilled by their sparkling beauty, but she was not inquisitive and never asked where they came from. The little waitress soon became a very rich woman. She furnished her flat beautifully and assured Pestek of her love. She said she adored him. Pestek told her about his home, his parents and siblings. Zosza listened with interest and swore that, should anything happen to him, she would send part of the treasures to his parents.

Lederer also had a secret that he did not share with Pestek. While in Birkenau, he had written to his friends in Theresienstadt. His message was a warning, concealed in the first letters of the words he wrote which ran as follows: *Gruesse alle Soehne. Tante und Onkel Doris.* (Greetings to all sons. Aunt and Uncle Doris.) He used an agreed upon code, but the addressees did not understand the meaning of the word *Gastod* (death by gas). Lederer had learned that from their reply. Now he had the opportunity to warn them personally. He planned to go to the ghetto of Theresienstadt.

He also had another journey on his mind—a journey to the only place that remained untouched by war—Switzerland.

Chapter 17

The Dealer in Documents

THE DAY OF THE appointment with Faltys came. Lederer and Pestek still had plenty of time when they reached Prague. Lederer wanted to see a friend who lived in Vinohrady, a Prague district. He arranged with Pestek to meet him at ten o'clock in front of the Old Town astronomical clock. He could not find his friend so he returned to the center of town, walking slowly down the Vaclavske namesti (Wenceslaus Square) and Mustek (little bridge). He turned right onto Rytirska Street toward Ovocny trh (fruit market). Then he saw a crowd of people in front of Celetna Street and spotted the police, who were closing all ways through to the Prasna brana (Powder Tower). He turned, but in the meantime the guards had also closed all passages into Zelezna Street. He looked for a way through. He tried to disappear through a passage, but even there he found a policeman. Lederer was trapped. He felt his blood pulsing in his temples. He was at a loss what to do next. A short while before he had felt safe with Welker's identity card in his pocket. Now he realized that without a work permit it was no good. He felt the pistol and the two grenades in his breast pockets. If worse came to worse, they were his only chance. That was a comfort.

It was half past eleven. Pestek would already be waiting in front of the astronomical clock. In half an hour, they both had a most important appointment, one that could not be postponed until a later date.

The police forced the crowd to line up. The head of the line was next to the Powder Tower. There the guards examined everyone's papers. Apparently they were looking for somebody in particular. Maybe for Lederer! The crowd got nearer and nearer the guards, and Lederer had to move with the line. He tried to think of what he could possibly do. He looked around. Just ordinary civilians, older men, worried women. No soldiers, officers, or anybody who looked like a German. He made up his mind. He quickly pinned a round badge with a swastika onto the lapel of his overcoat and the Iron Cross onto his tie. Then he started pushing toward the guards without regard for anybody. In front of the guards checking the papers, he started a quarrel with an old man.

"What's the matter?" a petty officer of the criminal police shouted. The incident made him stop his work. Lederer made his way to him through the crowd, lifted his right hand, and saluted: "Heil Hitler." Then he indignantly protested, "As a citizen of the Reich, I ask you to protect me against the insults of this rabble. I have an important commission in Berlin. My train leaves in twenty minutes. I ask you for protection. This is a priority case, and I ask you to handle it as such."

He was most determined about his complaint, and the policeman was impressed. The petty officer looked at Lederer attentively. His eyes rested on the Iron Cross on his tie. Lederer was unbuttoning his coat, seemingly searching for his identity card. The officer looked at him again, nodded benignly, and said, "It's all right. You may go."

Lederer saluted, thanked the officer, and proudly walked away, looking like a man satisfied that justice had been done. He went through Prikopy. He knew he had missed his appointment with Pestek, but he did not want to risk another such mishap.

He was seven minutes late for the second appointment in the lobby of the Hotel Sroubek at Vaclavske namesti. Gitta Skala met him impatiently. She introduced him to her friend and said reproachfully, "In another three minutes, we would have gone."

Mr. Faltys had a very good job. He was the dispatcher for a German transport agency named Kirchenberger. For three years he had been living on a volcano. He, like others, got used to it. His name used to be Feuerstein, but he changed it to Faltys and then dared take even bigger risks. He learned to be thorough like a German and cautious like a Czech.

Apart from his job, Mr. Faltys also had a small business of his own, as he was not obliged to spend all his time in his office. He rented a little grocery shop on one of the back streets of the Little Quarter of Prague from a couple named Trousil. Mrs. Trousil continued to sell goods in the shop, but her main task was to attend to the telephone and pass some strange messages. She often did not understand what she was talking about, but Mr. Faltys paid her well for her work. Mr. Trousil was a truck driver employed by the same firm as Faltys; Trousil's position in the company was somewhat inferior to that of Faltys. Trousil used to bring pork necks, ham, smoked meat, salami, and bacon from the nearby villages. He hid them in the body of the truck. This contraband was very useful because it could "soften up" even the most obstinate Nazi commanders. The goods were strictly rationed, but Trousil managed to get them nonetheless. Then he stored them behind Faltys's little shop. Mrs. Trousil distributed them as ordered by her boss. Faltys delivered even to the most destitute people in the German Reich—the pariahs in Theresienstadt. But he did not do it for nothing. The Faltys company received a constant supply of gold, money, diamonds, and other valuables from the hiding places in the ghetto, from the firearms house, from the gymnasium (Sokolovna), and from other hiding places that the Jews had used before the transports. Nor was that all. Faltys owned another business enterprise: a well-equipped workshop for producing all kinds of papers and documents.

Lederer watched and listened to Faltys, but could not make out what sort of a person he was. At first sight he did not look Jewish. He was gray at the temples, had a straight nose and brown eyes, and looked gentle and kind. He had a medium build and was well dressed. He gave the impression of a distinguished businessman.

"I suggest a walk in the park before we have our lunch," Faltys said, when they exchanged greetings. Gitta had informed Faltys of everything. Now Faltys verified the news from Auschwitz. He let Lederer relate the story of his escape and the plan for René's and her mother's breakout. Faltys loved risk and admired audacity. He seemed touched and prepared to help. Or at least that's how it appeared to Gitta, who thought she knew him well.

In front of Gitta, Faltys expressed his admiration for Lederer and Pestek. Then he dropped a few steps behind and silently considered the situation. Meanwhile Lederer talked to Gitta. When Faltys caught up with them, Lederer asked him again what he could do for them. He replied curtly and in a business-like manner, "I think I could provide reliable documents for you. They would cost 200,000 crowns per person."

Lederer was stunned. He was afraid he might never be able to scrape that much together. Faltys expected this reaction. He waited a little while, as if enjoying Lederer's embarrassment, and then continued, "I will take off half a million from the price if you will bring back from Auschwitz this young woman."

He handed Lederer a small photograph. On the back was written all the pertinent information.

"She went with the December transport, as you did, and she lives in the family camp. You can tell me during lunch what your decision is. Now let's have something to eat."

They had their lunch in a cozy little wine cellar near Petrin Park. Faltys ordered the best and most expensive food and drink. He did not hurry, but drew the lunch out as long as possible. He ordered dessert, fruit, coffee, cigars. He found an opportunity to whisper to the waiter, "Mr. Welker is a good friend of mine. I recommend him to you in case he needs anything. You'll look after him, won't you?"

"I would be honored." The waiter bowed to Lederer.

Faltys was good company. He was full of jokes. But Lederer was not in a jovial mood. He was sorry that Pestek was not with him. He did not know how this third escape could be arranged. Only four persons could fit in the car. Maybe Pestek would know what could be done. In the meantime there was no other way—he had to accept the offer. Even so, he did not know how he could scrape together the remaining 300,000 crowns. He could try and bargain with Faltys, to get him down. He could ask Gitta to help him. But Gitta and Faltys did not appear to be willing to discuss the matter; they had finished with it in the park.

Faltys paid an enormous sum for the dinner, and when Lederer thanked him, he said, "It's a small acknowledgment of your courage. And what have you decided to do?"

"To accept your offer. I will discuss the details with my colleague. When will the documents be ready for us?"

"We'll meet here in exactly ten days."

"And in case of a mishap?" Lederer asked cautiously.

"In that case I will leave a message here for you. You know the waiter."

Pestek looked for Lederer all over town. He was afraid of the worst—that Lederer had been picked up by the police. He did not want to take any further risk, so he returned to Zbraslav in the afternoon. The innkeeper introduced him to the local German elite, who were celebrating in the casino: a British cruiser had been sunk. Viktor soon forgot his worries and enjoyed himself with the Germans and their wives.

Lederer returned in the evening. Pestek was overjoyed to see him. He embraced him and introduced him as his friend and *Parteigenosse* (member of the party) Welker. He declared that his friend had been commissioned with a secret task connected with the maintenance of the dam in Stechovice.

Lederer's proper military behavior, his faultless Berlin accent, and the Iron Cross, combined with Pestek's story about a heroic deed in the Battle of Stalingrad, were most effective. It was quite a job, then, to get away from the company and to decline some sweet invitations from the Nazi womenfolk whose husbands were away at the front.

Walking through the woods toward the cottage, Lederer told Pestek what he had accomplished. When he spoke about Faltys's price and conditions, Pestek burst out indignantly, "That's blackmail and should be paid with a bullet."

"You are right, but we have no other chance. Do you think you could get yet another woman out of the camp?"

Pestek suggested several possibilities. He said it could be done, but exactly how would have to be decided when they got there. The main thing was to go and get René out as soon as possible. Then he asked impatiently, "When will he provide the papers?"

Lederer thought that this was the right moment to tell Pestek about his plans.

"In ten days. But you must not forget that we'll still have to pay 300,000 crowns."*

"Where will you get it from?"

"From the Theresienstadt ghetto. I have good friends there. I will warn them, and they'll help me."

"And what am I going to do?" Pestek asked, ill tempered.

"I will be back in a few days. Then we'll see."

---

* The equivalent of approximately $1,000 U.S currency at the time.

Chapter 18

Secretly in the Ghetto

IN A VILLAGE near Theresienstadt lived the barber Vaclav Vesely. He did not make enough money from his little shop to feed his four hungry children, therefore, he tried to earn a little extra. He organized a small village band, and they used to play at weddings, dances, and funerals. Now he was a little better off. He knew some police and went to shave them and cut their hair in the barracks of Theresienstadt.

It was the evening of April 20, 1944. Blazena Vesely was just putting the children to bed in their one-room flat. Her husband was tuning up his bass violin in the corner. Suddenly Vesely heard two knocks on the window. He leaned his instrument against the wall and stepped out of the house. Near the window was a man in a gray overcoat. He seemed familiar. Vesely approached and recognized the man who used to help him soap the beaver faces of the police in Theresienstadt.

"Siegfried! Where did you come from?" he cried out in surprise. He took Lederer in and asked many questions. Lederer knew that Vesely had often risked his life for the prisoners in Theresienstadt, but he did not want to make things too dangerous for him. So he did not tell him where he had come from and what he really intended to do.

"I left the ghetto without permission. I am late, and the guard who was to let me in is off duty now. You will have to show me a safe way through, Vaclav. I don't want to meet the guards."

Vesely had heard of such cases; Lederer was not the first, nor would he be the last. Still, it seemed strange that he had not seen him in the ghetto for such a long time. He went there every week, and once when he asked about Siegfried, he was told that he had left with a transport to the east. Lederer said the information was wrong: he had been punished and transferred. Now he was making wooden cases. The shop where he worked was in a tent in one of the Theresienstadt squares, and Lederer was not allowed to leave it during the day.

"Well, in that case we better go right now," Vesely said and brought the bicycles. In twenty minutes they covered the 7 kilometers to Theresienstadt. They stopped at the fence that bordered the military hospital. Vesely explained to Lederer how to proceed and what to avoid. Then he said, "I shall stay here and wait. If you can't get through, come back, and we'll find another way in." Vesely took a position at a tree, pretending to be repairing something on his bicycle, and followed Siegfried with his eyes.

Lederer took his shoes off and put them into his coat pockets. Then he snapped back the safety catch of his pistol and held it between his teeth. He stood still behind a tree, waiting for the right moment. He guessed that the distance to the nearest spot where he could hide was about 200 meters. The moon shone, the night was clear. Lederer was waiting for the guard to pass. As soon as he did, Lederer started running along the fence of the hospital and through some shrubbery that marked off the hospital grounds. A few yards before an enclosure he fell to the ground. He saw two small glowing lights between the trees that screened the fortress walls. Then he relaxed. The lights were just cigarettes, and they belonged to soldiers who were walking in the hospital park. Lederer was now only a few meters away from an enclosure where wood was stored. He sneaked along slowly, with his pistol in his mouth, one centimeter after another. As a boy he used to imagine Indians slinking like this to their enemies' settlements.

He reached the fence of the yard and watched a sentry walk in the moonlight on top of the fortress wall. The guard turned his back. Now! Lederer vaulted over the board fence and let himself down lightly into the yard, next to a pile of boards. One obstacle remained: the wire fence in front of the gymnasium. Lederer was watching a sentry who stood very close to him. The clouds just veiled the moon. Lederer slinked along in the darkness through the gymnasium yard and looked for a movable lattice in the fence. He found it, shifted it, and crept through the narrow opening.

He was in the ghetto. He straightened up, took the pistol out of his mouth, wiped it, and put it under his arm. He stood in an empty, desolate town; it looked as if under a spell. On a house he saw the familiar sign *Querstrasse* (transverse street). He sneaked along the row of houses till he found 18 Langstrasse, where his friend lived. He opened the front door as quietly as he could and went upstairs on tip-toe. The chief of the fire brigade used to live here. Leo Holzer had made a flat for himself of 10 square meters in the attic. The flat was divided into several parts by embrasures. The light came through little dormer windows. He had made a tiny place, where he had some privacy, out of boards, pasteboard boxes, straightened tin barrels, and old fire hoses.

The dim light of a lamp made it possible for Lederer to see a little. He saw the familiar broken glass in the door. It was glued together with newspaper on both sides. He knocked.

"Who is it?" a frightened voice asked after a while.

"It's me, Siegfried. Open the door, Leo."

Even in the dim light it was possible to see part of Holzer's flat through the chinks between the boards. Two berths, walls made of un-planed planks, partly covered with a cloth. Wooden crates instead of chairs. Embroidered coverlets hanging on the walls, a nice striped curtain, and colored pillows on the seats disclosed that there must be a woman living in this attic, trying to make it as cozy as possible.

A tall, slim figure, lying on the lower berth, threw back his blanket, got down, and came to the door. On the upper berth, a tuft of black hair and a pair of surprised eyes could be seen from under the blanket. Leo Holzer, with an oil lamp in his hand, turned the nail that served as a lock. He opened it a little and threw the light on his visitor's face. He was so surprised that he could not utter a word. He took Lederer in his arms and hugged him. Mariana, his wife, jumped down from her berth and greeted him cordially.

"How did you get here, Siegfried?" Holzer said at last.

"I flew away from Auschwitz," Lederer said simply, as if it were an everyday occurrence. Lederer sat down on one of the wobbly crates.

"Send for the boys," Lederer said. "I don't want to repeat everything more than once."

Holzer put on his coat and quietly went downstairs. In a little while guests started flocking in, staring at Lederer. The first was George Petschauer of the *Ghettowache*. Then Fischer from the Transport Administration, Schliesser from Economic Management, and Sax from the locksmith workshop. The last to come was the rabbi, a member of the Elder's Council. They drew the table near the bunk bed, put the crates together, and sat down on them, as well as on the edge of the bed. Then they listened silently to every word of what Lederer had to say. He seemed to them a strange messenger from another world. They had received letters from that other world, but they had never seen anybody return from it. Lederer produced some cigarettes, cigars, and matches and put them on the table. They all started smoking. And Lederer started talking . . .

There was a gloomy look on the faces of the seven men, and a heavy, sad atmosphere settled on the room, as if they were saying a prayer for the dead. Every one of the listeners had wanted to ask about his own family, but now all such questions seemed to be petty and superfluous.

Petschauer broke the silence. "What shall we do?"

"Carry on for the dead in Birkenau; do what they could not do themselves. Prevent the transports and prepare a rebellion."

Without further hesitation Lederer said, "Set the ghetto on fire."

"And what about the fire guards?" Holzer asked, alarmed.

"They will put out the fire with oil and petrol," Lederer answered, smiling.

"What if the SS shoot us all?" Schliesser objected, frightened.

"Then we would not have to die in Birkenau," Sax, the locksmith, replied.

"How can you think of a rebellion with old men and women? Seventy-five percent of the people in the ghetto are over sixty-five!" said Fischer, who worked in the statistics department.

"All the better," Petschauer snapped. "All we have to do is put the straw sacks on fire; just a few liters of petrol, some rags, oil, and a handful of brave boys from the fire guards and from the *Ghettowache*. The Germans will think twice before they slaughter everybody in this privileged ghetto, the town that has been given to the Jews by the Fuehrer."

They quietly discussed what to do and how to inform the people of Theresienstadt about what was happening in Auschwitz and Birkenau without risking disclosure of their plan or panic. They also discussed how further transports could be prevented. Lederer suggested he try to get in touch with a group of partisans in the Brdy woods southwest of Prague and damage the railway bridge near Bohusovice. He had heard about the partisans' activities from Mican and felt sure that the group from Zbraslav would help.

The gloomy mood that had prevailed in the little room an hour before changed into a spirit of resistance and daring. They were full of hope. They realized that a rebellion in the Theresienstadt ghetto would have international repercussions and would affect public opinion more than the Jewish rebellion in Warsaw the year before. The Nazis were retreating under the pressure of the Soviet army on all fronts.

The only one who had not spoken was the rabbi. Now he turned to Lederer with his grave, searching look.

"You said that the youth leader, the teacher of our children in Theresienstadt, perished on the eighth of March?"

"Yes," Lederer assured him, "he committed suicide when he saw that he had been deceived and that it was too late to resist."

"That's impossible. I don't believe it." The rabbi handed a typed letter to Lederer. "Just read the copy of a report that was sent by Fred Hirsch to Switzerland at the end of February about the education of our children in Birkenau. He also enclosed some of their drawings. Look, here they are. And here," the rabbi went on, pointing with a trembling finger at the date of a postcard that he was showing to Lederer. "Fred wrote to me on the twenty-fifth of March. I received it a week ago."

Lederer felt sorry for the dignified, trusting man, who was so proud of his gifted pupils. He looked around and his eyes rested on Schliesser, who was enjoying one of Pestek's cigars. He then turned to the rabbi, pointed to the ashy cigar in Schliesser's mouth, and said, "Look at the cigar, rabbi.* It still holds the form of something that does not exist anymore, just as the people who came from Theresienstadt do not live in Birkenau anymore, even though they still exist."

The men started leaving in the early hours of the morning. Lederer promised to carry out letters and messages for them on his way back. He was dead tired. The Holzers invited him to stay with them. In the afternoon Petschauer brought some plans of the Nazi espionage archives, which had been transferred to the Sudeten barracks after the first bombing of Berlin. Holzer showed Lederer some reports that had been sent abroad through the police and civilians for enormous bribes. None of these reports had ever been acknowledged. Lederer told them that he was thinking of going to Switzerland, and they were thrilled to hear it. They wrote a short account of the conditions in the ghetto and added plans of the layout of the Nazi archive.

It seemed that Holzer and his friends were in touch with the partisans in the Zbraslav region. They even knew Mican. Lederer learned from

---

* According to Leo Holzer's testimony this man was the noted rabbi Leo Beck, deported from Berlin to Theresienstadt. An explanation for his passive attitude may be found in Jacob Robinson's introduction to Isaiah Trunk's book *Judenrat* (New York: Stein & Day, 1972), p. XXXI: "In Theresienstadt Leo Beck followed a policy of nonrevelation in view of his judgement that nothing could have been done to change the course of events. It was—in his view—advisable not to let victims know the truth and to spare them the agony and ultimate desperation that comes from knowledge that the end is near and there is absolutely no way out."

them that Mican was a friend of an official responsible for sending men to work in the Reich. They also discussed the possibilities of getting the money for Faltys. They did not have ready cash in the ghetto, but they could supply addresses of reliable people who kept money and valuables for them in Prague. Lederer promised to bring arms and spare parts for their wireless set.

In the evening there was another gathering at Holzers, but with different people. The first reaction to Lederer's news was distrust. Their most important arguments were the postcards received from the *Arbeitslager Birkenau bei Neu-Berun.* They had been written by the relatives that Lederer reported to be dead. Only recently a courier from Berlin had brought a heap of postcards from Auschwitz-Birkenau to the post office in Theresienstadt. They came, as did all the other letters addressed for the prisoners, from the *Reichsvereinigung der Juden in Deutschland Berlin* (the Reich Union of Jews in Germany), an association of Jews organized by the Nazis.

Lederer spent one more night in Holzer's flat. Then, burdened down with letters, like a postman, he started out from the ghetto two hours before dawn. He left the same way he had come.

He reached Travcice in the early hours of the morning. The barber's family was still asleep. Only Vesely was up.

"Why did you come back so soon?" he asked, surprised.

"I must tell you the truth, Vaclav. I fled from Auschwitz and went to warn the boys in Theresienstadt."

Vesely listened to what Lederer had to say. When he finished, Vesely said, "I can't believe that men can be such beasts!"

"They said the same thing in the ghetto. They just don't understand the danger they are in. One short visit is not enough. I'll have to be back again. Will you be afraid to help me knowing what you do now?"

Vesely thought for a moment. "I have a wife and four children. I'll have to think of them very hard when I shave the SS beasts, or else my razor may slip. I'll do what I can for you, Siegfried. If we don't stop them now, it will soon be our turn. When they finish with the Jews, they'll butcher us all."

Then he took the bicycle and saw Lederer to the train in Bohusovice. His wife was waiting for him when he got back. She had heard them talking in the morning and had reproached him, insisting that he should think of his family first. She pointed at the sleeping children and said, "Are you not afraid of what might happen to our children, Vaclav? The Gestapo are all around; if they hear anything, they will do away with us all."

"We'll have to be very careful," Vesely said. And that was all that was said about it.

Chapter 19

Message to Switzerland

ON HIS WAY BACK, Lederer stayed in Prague to mail the letters, deliver the messages, see the people who kept the valuables, and arrange with them when and where they would be available. In the afternoon he arrived in Zbraslav. The innkeeper prevailed upon Lederer to give an account of Auschwitz, of the escape, and of their rescue plan to a small group of partisans in a well-secured back room.

"We have already heard something about the gas chambers broadcast from abroad. But it was too awful, too unconvincing. We could not believe it," said one of the partisans after Lederer's account.

"That's the trouble," said Lederer. "Only an eyewitness can convince people about what the Nazis are doing, and only an eyewitness can arouse and stir the world to do something about it."

It was nearly midnight when the partisans left the room. Only the innkeeper remained. Lederer delivered greetings from the ghetto, and he ended his report by saying, "I would like to bring their report, and mine, to Switzerland and deliver it personally to the International Red Cross."

"How do you propose to get there?" asked Mican.

"Germany borders Switzerland in the south and west. Surely along such a long stretch of land there must be a place where I could cross the frontier. It would be enough to get officially into the Reich. I was told in Theresienstadt that people are sent there from here by the local authorities."

"I will introduce you to Pepik Pokorny. He knows all about it," said the innkeeper.

The next day Mican introduced Lederer to Pokorny. "Do you know this man from Plzen?" Mican asked Pokorny.

And when Pokorny replied, "Yes, I know him. He lived in the same street at number 29," Lederer knew that Pokorny belonged to a subdivision of Weidman's group called Plzenak 28. Pokorny was now an official of the Zbraslav Town Council.

The three of them had supper together. Pokorny listened breathlessly when Lederer told him about the death factory in Auschwitz. He forgot about eating and drinking. He asked many questions, and Lederer explained everything.

"Yes," Pokorny confirmed, "they spoke about it on the wireless from Moscow, as well as from London, but they would have to explain it like you, Siegfried, for people to believe it. What can we do for you?"

"He needs to get somewhere near the German-Swiss border," said Mican. And Lederer told him about his plans.

Just then somebody knocked three times on the door. Mican left, and when he returned, he said, "Pepik, you must go right now to meet Jicha at the Hotel Prochazka."

Pokorny put out his hand to Lederer and said, "We'll meet here in two days, Siegfried."

In front of the hotel, Pokorny spotted a German truck. Behind it was Jicha, the chief of the local police, armed with a rifle. He grinned and said in a low voice, "The two officers are having a good time. They are talking to the girls in the pub, and the driver went to fetch them. There are some cases full of hand grenades in the van."

Pokorny quickly climbed up on the back of the truck, removed a small but heavy case, hid it under his coat, and carried it away to Mican's barn.

Pepik Pokorny was in charge of the Zbraslav regional welfare and police departments. His colleagues were Jicha, the chief of the police, and Jira, the manager of the labor office. Both of them, as well as Mican, had belonged to Weidman's resistance group. After some of the members in Plzen were imprisoned, the group in Zbraslav started working on their own. They secured information about the equipment and production in factories controlled by the Nazis. They poured sugar into the petrol tanks of Nazi cars and trucks and sand into the bearings of railway cars on the Zbraslav railway station. Jicha covered them and warned them when necessary. He also "searched" for the offenders when he received orders from Prague to investigate the sabotage actions.

Pokorny went to see him the day after he spoke to Lederer. Many applications for workers came to Jira's labor office; they were from the German firms, who looked for specialists from other nations because their own were dying on the battlefields. The offices in the Protectorate of Bohemia and Moravia were ordered to send every person who was not indispensable to the Reich. The strict orders were not always obeyed, especially lately, and thus Jira, with Pokorny, could pick the specialists themselves. They also equipped them and then sent them to Germany. Now they looked through the applications. Pokorny took one of them, and in the evening, he discussed it with Lederer.

"A German firm needs an engineering specialist urgently. It's a shipbuilding plant in Constance. It is located at Constance Lake, and on the other side of the lake is Switzerland. That's just what you need, Siegfried."

Lederer had not dared dream of an opportunity that would fit his plans so perfectly. They discussed the details and agreed that he would get his papers for the journey to Constance through Jira. The papers would be in the name of Welker.

Lederer returned to the cabin just before midnight. He found it empty. Pestek returned from Prague the next morning. He poured out of his briefcase more booty: a pistol, grenades, tins of food, and much-longed-for binoculars. He told Lederer all about his adventures and how he'd stolen the goods. He admitted that it was very risky. In one of the pubs a plainclothes Gestapo agent asked to see his papers. Pestek answered with a punch. They fought, and Pestek knocked him out. In the melée that followed, he ran out. Lederer followed the story with interest, but it was evident that he was not very enthusiastic.

Pestek, on the other hand, showed no understanding for Lederer's strange excursions. He was afraid that the more connections they had, the greater the risk of disclosure. He was convinced that he was doing more for their cause by providing arms, food, and papers than Siegfried, who allowed Faltys to blackmail him. That man deserved to be done away with. Pestek was afraid of Lederer's secret connections. He felt that they jeopardized his only desire and aim in life—to be with René and wait with her for the end of the war. When Lederer reprimanded him for drawing the attention of the police and the Gestapo with unnecessary escapades, Pestek lost control.

"And what about you?" Pestek burst out. "You go and warn the Jews in the ghetto! What's the use of it? Do you think you can save them? You think they will believe you in Theresienstadt, 500 kilometers away from Auschwitz, when they did not believe it even in Birkenau, 500 meters away from the gas chambers? Where they can't sleep because of the flames rising from the chimneys, and where they drink the ashes of the dead in their water and swallow them with every piece of food?"

Lederer had to agree with him, but he was afraid of admitting to himself how disappointed he had been at Holzer's when the people chose to believe the posthumous postcards rather than his eyewitness account. But he did not admit that to Pestek.

"They believed me!" he said. "I explained the trick with the postcards. They will not be deceived again. They will not go like cattle to be slaughtered. They will rebel and defend themselves!"

"Defend themselves? But how?" Pestek asked. "It is not as simple as that! It's not the same as when David fought Goliath! You prisoners talk about resistance and rebellion all the time, but you haven't a single rifle, a single gun, and you don't know how to fight! How can defenseless and wretched prisoners resist or revolt successfully against the German war machine, which has been fighting the whole world these last five years?"

"The Nazis will lose the war," Lederer protested. "They are already nearing the end. The Russians are advancing. The British have chased the Germans out of Africa. The Americans are bombing their towns. And their allies are giving up."

"Yes, you are right, they are losing," Pestek admitted, "the Nazis have lost already. In and out of their country. But they are still kicking; they still have armies, concentration camps, factories. Goebbels has promised that everything will change again when a new, miraculous weapon is introduced by the Fuehrer. One aircraft, one squad with guns and flamethrowers would be sufficient to liquidate the whole ghetto in Theresienstadt. In one day the Nazis can silence those who behave like sheep, just like those who rebel!

"You are a dreamer, Siegfried," Pestek went on. "You have lost your sense of reality. You don't see our situation correctly. We can hardly help those closest to us. We can't save them all. Do you want to play the savior?"

Lederer knew that Pestek was interested only in his own happiness and would not hear about anything else. They had discussed the situation many times. They had asked themselves who was guilty, why the German people did not rise and overthrow the hateful Fuehrer and his regime. He again tried to explain where he saw the root of the evil.

"The whole world is fighting against fascism. The prisoners must not stand aloof from this struggle, even when they are behind barbed wire."

"But what is fascism?" Pestek said. "Why is it so strong and attractive? How do you explain why it has been so powerful for such a long time?"

"Fascism is inhuman and selfish. It stands for hatred and evil, and its culmination is Auschwitz. If a regime that intentionally encourages the lowest instincts in men, makes them flourish, and awards them as virtues—if that regime seizes power, then the evil becomes the new order. That's the Nazi regime. It divides men into castes, robs them of the fruits of their work, and destroys them like worms. You have yourself experienced how you have been made into robots, unconditionally obedient, mercilessly killing anybody marked as an enemy. None of you has dared to protest, even when you knew and realized that those whom you were ordered to kill were blameless and harmless, honest and respectable people. All of you knew no pity or any human feelings!"

"You are sermonizing like Jesus Christ to the Apostles," Pestek said, "but this reality is different, and we have to live in it. Those who are hard and selfish, who pay no heed, those are the ones who win! For instance, look at my Iron Cross! What do you think I got it for? For a murder! For not staying in the shelter when the Russians smashed my gun, but killing a few Russian soldiers with a bundle of hand grenades. None of them ever harmed me. They had families, they loved their lives, they defended their country. The commander of Auschwitz was awarded a medal for a record number of assembly-line murders. The front officers get promoted for successfully forcing the soldiers into lost and nonsensical battles. The less humanity, the more suffering, the more dead, the bigger the promotion and glory. How do you fight against fascism, whose basic idea is brutality, in a world that is ruled by principles of brutality and where merit is measured by the amount of brutality?"

"There are other people besides Fascists in the world," Lederer insisted patiently. "Not even all the Germans are Nazis. Only a small segment of mankind has become infected by fascism. You must not be confused by their power. It's only an illusion, based on cruelty, terror, and ruthlessness. But, in the end, the heart and reason will decide whether the finger on the trigger will murder, or whether it will protect. I went to the ghetto to warn the people of Theresienstadt, to encourage and to convince them that they have to defend themselves against brutality, even if it seems hopeless. You are a good example, Viktor. You have come over to the side of freedom and humanity in spite of the fact that you are risking your life."

Pestek did not say anything and sat considering Lederer's last words. Lederer saw that this was the right moment to gain Pestek's agreement for the journey he was planning with Pokorny. He went on after a while, "It's not enough to inform and rouse the isolated and defenseless. We have seen everything with our own eyes, and therefore we have to tell the world what is meant by the words *final solution.*"

"Whom do you propose to inform and warn?" asked Pestek.

"The International Red Cross in Geneva, in whose name the Nazis have been deceiving the world and murdering thousands of people."

"Do you think that they don't know about it in Geneva? You think it will help?" Pestek was full of doubts.

"We must all make our own contribution, or else there will be no end to the secret gas war. If the gentlemen in the biggest humanitarian organization do not want to listen and understand, then they will just be digging their own graves—and the graves of all mankind as well."

Pestek realized that it was not only his love for René, but the crematoriums and the gas chamber as well that had brought him to the other side. He remembered the fighting and suffering of the German soldiers on the eastern front and knew that there was no mercy, no compromise in this fight. Yet, he still did not like Lederer's plan. A trip to Constance and from there a search for a connection to the International Red Cross in Geneva seemed too risky to him.

"With the papers you have, you won't be able to get to Switzerland. The borders are exceptionally well guarded. The Nazi intelligence service and the counterespionage people check the documents at the border. You will arouse suspicion; not to speak of your documents, which won't hold up to close scrutiny. And even if you cross the border, you will be followed. They may detain you, and that would be the end of our plans," concluded Pestek.

"But it is of utmost importance that the International Red Cross get an eyewitness report about what is going on in Auschwitz. It is my duty to go there," Lederer said. "So far the Nazis have managed to fool all the international commissions and, as you well know, the mass extermination goes on without any interference from the outside world."

"Do you have reliable contacts or friends in Constance—or anywhere in Switzerland, for that matter—like you have in Prague, or in Plzen, or in Theresienstadt?" Pestek asked pointedly. "You don't know anybody there, and the company to which you are sent from the labor office will check you thoroughly. They will follow your every step. Moreover, my leave is almost over. You can hardly be back by then, and if I'm not back in Auschwitz in time, they will start investigations. Think it over, Siegfried. It's too risky, too dangerous.

Can't you think of another way to send your message? Isn't there a Swiss consulate in Prague, or somewhere in Slovakia?"

Lederer had to admit that he hadn't considered all the possible complications and dangers connected with his planned trip to Switzerland. His enthusiasm for the journey to Constance slowly faded as he listened to Pestek's objections.

Pestek is right, he thought. He would go to Prague. He would write a report about Auschwitz and somehow pass it to the Swiss consulate in Prague. Anyway, he had to go to Prague to find the people who were entrusted with the money that belonged to his friends in Theresienstadt.

It took Lederer two days to write a convincing report about all that was happening in Auschwitz. He drew a detailed sketch of the concentration camps and of all the annihilation installations, along with a legend and explanatory notes. Pestek, who intimately knew the entire complex of the Auschwitz camps, helped him draw the map in the correct proportions. They took special care to locate properly the exact site of the furnaces and their distance from the railway station.

Equipped with these documents, Lederer left for Prague. In the telephone directory he found the number of the Swiss consulate. He dialed and the secretary who answered the phone told him that the consul was very busy. He managed to persuade her that he had a very urgent and important message that must be delivered personally. The secretary explained that the consul was out of town, but told Lederer when his deputy might be reached in his office.

Lederer went straight to the consulate. He stopped some distance away and watched the entrance for a while. Apart from a uniformed officer of the *Sicherheitpolizei* (security police), Lederer noticed two other plainclothes policemen. The people who attempted to enter the consulate were stopped by the uniformed officer and had to produce their identification papers. The officer examined them carefully and wrote down the identity card numbers in his notebook. Lederer went to a nearby café, where he could keep watch of the consulate entrance. He noticed that some of the people who left the building were followed by the plainclothes police. He came to the conclusion that it would be too risky for him to enter. He paid for his coffee and went to the post office to phone Gitta Skala. She agreed to come to Prague immediately, by the afternoon train. Lederer met her at the railway station and took her to his room in the Hotel Sroubek to explain the situation.

Gitta understood what had to be done. She took Lederer's report and the maps he had drawn and promised she would find a way to deliver them to the consul himself. She also gave Lederer useful instructions for dealing with Faltys. Then she took the midnight train back to Plzen.

Lederer knew he had nothing to worry about. Gitta Skala was reliable. His report would be delivered.

He spent another three days in Prague contacting the people who were safeguarding his friends' money. Lederer needed the money urgently to pay for the forged documents. Some of the people told him that during house searches the Gestapo had confiscated the money and jewels, but in most cases, everything went smoothly. He managed to get together about 100,000 Czech crowns, two diamond bracelets, and three gold rings with precious stones.

Chapter 20

The Auschwitz Railway Station

PESTEK WAS ELATED when he saw Lederer enter Mican's inn. He admitted how afraid he had been. Lederer might not have come back from his risky undertaking, and Pestek would have been lost, all alone in a foreign country. His daring and thefts had been reported to the police. Plainclothes as well as uniformed spies were now much more exacting in controlling nightclubs and bars. Pestek had recently made another nighttime excursion, despite his promise to Lederer not to do so. This time he had only just escaped.

The following day Lederer and Pestek hurried to reach their appointment on time. Faltys, clean-shaven and in a stylish new suit, was waiting for them. He sat at the table by himself, without Gitta Skala this time. He waved at the newcomers in a friendly manner and invited them to have lunch with him. As Faltys made small talk, Lederer began to get nervous. He hinted at the problem of the papers, but Faltys tried to avoid answering. He talked about the difficulties and penalties of other such offenses recently disclosed. Lederer then got straight to the point.

"My friend Pestek has come to tell you about his plans for the liberation of your protegée from the family camp in Auschwitz."

Pestek explained his plan. They would ask the transport department of the SS *Fahrbereitschaft* in Auschwitz for a car in order to take prisoners from the Czech Family Camp for supposed cross-examination as ordered by the Gestapo. They would dispose of the driver and thus gain a place for Faltys's protegée.

Faltys listened halfheartedly while Pestek talked about the details of the assault and seemed to be absorbed in other thoughts. Suddenly he raised his hand and stopped Pestek in mid-sentence. "You know, gentlemen, I am not so sure that this plan will be any good. Intrigues of this sort are no good with the Germans. They have to be tackled in an entirely different way!"

He then told them that he had contacted a retired German general who had access to Goering and Eichmann. He was a relative of the Prague Emigration Center commander, who disposes of the prisoners in Theresienstadt and in the family camp in Birkenau. He had advanced the sum of half a million crowns to the general for the release of his relative. Therefore, he now had no money for the documents for Lederer and Pestek. Furthermore, he could not take anything less than the full amount, and only if they could pay a really large sum of money would he risk it again. He would do it only for the sake of Miss Skala and her dear late father.

Lederer thought of what Pestek had told him about Faltys and now completely agreed with him. This was blackmail. Faltys did not deserve anything but death. His eyes met Pestek's. They were both thinking the same thing.

Faltys, as if he knew what they felt, said, "I know this is a difficult position for you, and I won't leave you in the lurch." He produced some papers out of his black leather briefcase. They were birth and domicile certificates for René Karen and her mother. They looked quite genuine.

"A hundred and fifty thousand crowns for all." Then he presented a few note papers with the letterhead of the *Reichsicherheithauptamt* (RSHA, Head Office of the Reich Police) in Berlin. "Ten thousand apiece," he said.

Lederer was fuming. Pestek was waiting for a sign from him. But Faltys knew what was in their minds. He pressed his body against Lederer and made sure he could feel the hard metal object hidden under his arm. Then he said, "You think it's a lot for perfect Aryan papers and blank stationery that will make it possible for you to achieve even the impossible?"

Lederer was weighing his options. He would have loved to have throttled this bloodsucker, but he suppressed his rage. Calmly, he produced the bank notes from his wallet and then the rings and diamonds. He presented the money to Faltys and said, "That's all the fugitives from Auschwitz can offer."

Faltys' face remained impassive. He counted the notes.

"A hundred thousand," he stated. Then he examined the diamonds and rings through a magnifying glass. He estimated them at 70,000. Lederer gave a nod, and Faltys gave him the folder with the documents and added two blank sheets with the RSHA letterhead.

Two days later Lederer went to Theresienstadt again. This time he brought the promised spare parts and arms with him. Four pistols were from Mican and Pokorny. Lederer had been astonished when he had seen the arsenal in Mican's barn.

"Where did you get them from?" he had asked.

"That's a secret, but I will tell *you*, Siegfried," Pokorny said. "When the Nazis came to Czechoslovakia, they issued a decree that all arms were to be surrendered. The citizens of Zbraslav delivered them to me. I asked everybody whether they had a gun license. If someone did not and was a reliable person, I said it was all right and put the arms aside."

Mican also gave Lederer medicine. "You can say in the ghetto that these are from the pharmacist of Zbraslav."

Lederer went by train. In Travcice he waited until it was dark and then, with Vasely's help, he found his way into Theresienstadt. In the ghetto they were surprised at Lederer's accomplishments and ashamed at the same time, because they had the same connections and had not dared use them. Lederer told them about Faltys. Petschauer and Holzer were not surprised. They too had to rely on such ruthless people. They had no choice. Faltys was one of the few who managed to get medicine from abroad.

"Soon we must go back to Auschwitz, and our papers are still far from perfect," Lederer said. "Do you know anybody who is not such a rogue?"

"I do," said Holzer, "he's in our fire guard brigade, and he worked for many years in the Neubert publishing house in Prague. He is an off-setting expert."

They called Pavel Berger. Lederer showed him the papers that Pestek had collected during his nighttime adventures and told him what should be done with them. Berger looked at them carefully and said, "I'd need tools and material. George Adler is the only person who could get them for me here in the ghetto."

Adler was the head of an art department, which had ten members and worked under the direct control of the SS. Other prisoners were not allowed to enter the workshop. Only a few prisoners—goldsmiths, photographers, designers, and such—were chosen to make art objects and souvenirs: jewelry, pictures, engravings. They repaired and renovated art objects and pictures that had been brought from elsewhere. So Holzer went to Adler. He did not tell him what the tools were for, but brought most of what Berger needed. In a little closet in the attic of the fire station, Berger fixed the papers for Lederer and Pestek in two days.

It was the end of May 1944. On June 20, the six-month quarantine period of the December transport would end. Pestek was anxious to fulfill his plan for saving René as soon as possible. Lederer had to go to Plzen once more. He had to consult with Faltys and could find him only through Gitta Skala.

As they arranged, he met her at a bus stop. She was terrified; apparently she was being watched. She whispered that Faltys had been arrested. The Gestapo had found out about him and taken him to Pankrac Prison.

"You must disappear," she warned him and got onto the bus. Lederer didn't dare go anywhere else and left Plzen immediately.

He felt better in the cabin in Zbraslav. There he and Pestek were safe. There they prepared for their journey.

On the evening of May 25, two SS officers in well-pressed uniforms got onto the international express train, Prague-Bohumin-Warsaw. Lederer (SS Obersturmfuehrer Welker) and Pestek (SS Untersturmfuehrer Hauser) carried a letter from the RSHA that commissioned them to fetch and question two women prisoners from Auschwitz camp B-II-b. They traveled without incident in a first-class compartment. They again checked and completed all the details of the rescue and return journey.

In Cidice they changed to the familiar train to Auschwitz. Pestek contemplated whether he should go on to Myslowice in order to reclaim his treasure from Zosza, his mistress. Lederer tried to dissuade him, but Pestek was convinced it was a good idea.

"When we get out with René, we'll need it," he said. "Where will we get money from? Wasn't our experience with Faltys enough? Shall I throw my own belongings away, when they are within easy reach?"

When they came to the town of Auschwitz, Lederer got ready to alight. Pestek decided to go to Myslowice, although warned against it by Lederer. He shook hands with his partner and said, "We should not do anything in Auschwitz today anyway. I'll be back from Myslowice tomorrow. Meet me at the night train."

Lederer got off. He went through the streets of the town and found accommodations at a hotel. In the morning, he checked around the town and learned that nothing had changed in the family camp. He rang up the SS *Fahrbereitschaft* (transport department). The officer confirmed that there would be a car at his disposal. He again checked the whole plan. Everything seemed to be going well. He returned to the hotel, ordered a glass of vodka, and asked for the railway timetable. He looked for the evening train from Myslowice. A quarter of an hour before its scheduled arrival he was waiting for Pestek on the ramp.

Shortly before the train arrived, he heard the roar of motorcycles. They stopped in front of the building. A dozen armed SS soldiers emerged from the dust. They closed the railway station and forced all passengers into the waiting room. An assault squad occupied the platform.

As the train came into the station, Lederer could see Pestek leaning out of the window, looking for him. The commander of the squad apparently recognized him. He jumped up on the steps of Pestek's car and Lederer heard a shot. A grenade exploded on the platform among the SS. Lederer seized the opportunity. He made for the motorcycles in front of the station. They were not being watched. He mounted the first in the row, started the engine, and accelerated. In forty minutes he reached the Czech frontier, 50 kilometers from Auschwitz. As he drove through the village, he saw a policeman signaling him to stop. He bent his head to the handles, accelerated, and went by him. The guards at the frontier did not stop the SS Obersturmfuehrer's motorcycle. When Lederer reached Bohumin, he put the motorcycle in a driveway, asked the way to the railway station, and bought his ticket back to Prague.

Lederer had not seen the events at the railway platform clearly, and no witness could be found to describe what had happened. Most likely, Pestek's visit to Zosza in Myslowice had been betrayed, as she had contacts with other SS from Birkenau. Lederer had no way of finding out what had happened to Pestek but in Birkenau and later, among some of the survivors, confused rumors circulated that Pestek had been caught and killed.

Some years later I had contact with my countryman and Auschwitz friend Josef Neumann, who had moved to the United States after the war. During my visit to the U.S. in 1978 Neumann granted me an interview, which I quote from below:*

"On the morning of May 26, 1944, I was going through the camp gate, when an SS barracks leader came up and searched me thoroughly. I felt him shove a note into my pocket, which turned out to be from Pestek, telling me when and where to meet him. I went to the unfinished 'Mexico' camp in section B-III and in the barracks indicated on the note found Pestek hiding in the attic, pointing two revolvers at me.

" 'Maybe now you'll trust me,' he said and pulled me up into the loft with him. I embraced him, for his return seemed miraculous. He was wearing an SS Untersturmfuehrer's uniform, looked completely exhausted, his hair was a mess, and he was unshaven. He told me, 'If you want to come with me, get ready; we leave at 10:30.' I think he had a car behind the camp. He asked me to see that René from the Czech Family Camp was also ready. It was probably mainly on her account that he had dared return to Birkenau. The whole meeting lasted barely two minutes.

"I was on my way to the appointed place at the agreed upon time, fully prepared for flight. But when I was still some way off I noticed something unusual going on at the barracks where Pestek was hiding. He had been betrayed and was surrounded by SS. I could not go back, so I continued on to the Czech Family Camp to warn René. Here I quickly got rid of everything I was carrying, especially the civilian clothing.

"Scarcely had I done this when I heard them looking for me all over the camp. Three SS members who were especially known for their brutality, one on a motorcycle, were combing the camp, searching every block. Their first question when they found me was, 'Where's Pestek?'

" 'I don't know,' I said, an answer that immediately cost me two teeth. They kicked me along the guardroom, where I saw Pestek hanging by his wrists from the bars of the window. He was so bloody

* Neumann was born in Snina, Slovakia. He was deported in April 1942 to Auschwitz and tattooed with the number 29867. He testified on the Lederer-Pestek escape at the great Auschwitz trial before the German court in Frankfurt/Main on November 26, 1964. For more on this topic see B. Naumann's book *Auschwitz* (Frankfurt: Atheneum Verlag, 1965), pp. 392-93.

from beatings that he was barely recognizable. They tied me by my wrists to the other window and left us alone together for a while, hoping perhaps to overhear our conversation through the door.

"I was then interrogated by Schwarzhuber, the camp commander. They got nothing out of me. Then they tied Pestek and me together and dragged us to the notorious block no. 11 at the Auschwitz main camp, where people slated for execution were held. It must have been a grim sight as the bleeding SS officer and the Jewish prisoner, lashed together, entered the block from which few ever came out alive. Pestek and I were separated and thrown into solitary confinement. My hands were tied together and were only freed when they brought me food. Every day I heard them assembling the prisoners to be shot, every shot in the courtyard signaling the death of a comrade.

"Jakub Kozelczik, the Jewish prison Kapo, searched me thoroughly when I entered the prison and removed all contraband. Jakub gave me daily reports on what was happening with Pestek, and once he let me briefly meet with Pestek in his cell. He looked bad, cruelly treated. He only said, 'I disclosed nobody. Lederer is okay.' Kozelczik, who had experience and connections, kept trying to convince me that he could save my life if I paid a considerable sum to the SS dealing with the case. With Jakub's help I obtained the money from my friends in the camp, and he paid it secretly to the SS as a ransom.

"Pestek was interrogated viciously for about a month, undergoing fearful torture and violence. He was sentenced by SS Polizeigericht Katowice to death and was shot. All those who knew of my case found it incredible that I should have escaped with my life, much less been sent back to Birkenau. No one could imagine the ghastly uncertainty and terror I endured as I walked back to Birkenau, accompanied by SS, along the road leading to both the camp and the crematoriums and gas chambers. We passed the men's quarantine camp, the Czech Family Camp, the Hungarian camp, the *Stammlager* (men's camp), and reached the place where the road divided. To my immense relief and surprise, we turned not toward the crematoriums, but in the direction of the Birkenau Gestapo guardroom in the former Gypsy camp (B-II-e). The SS officers welcomed me with a sound beating and sent me off to penal block no. 11 in the men's camp (B-II-d). I did not have to go to work. Instead I had to report every day to the political department of the Gestapo, where they tried to get me to confess. For a full two weeks they tried every kind of torture and ill treatment, which culminated in their slamming the door on my fingers, whereupon I fainted.

"My principal tormentors were SS Rottenfuehrers Broad and Lachmann. Then for a while they changed tactics and treated me unexpectedly well, plying me with cigarettes and suggestions that I should cooperate with them by spying on their behalf in the camp. When I refused they turned violent again, and so it went for five more weeks. But I told them nothing.

"From Jakub we learned how Pestek had fearlessly threatened the SS who questioned him, for he knew a great deal about most of them. Thus he had to be silenced. Their objective in keeping me alive was to be a living witness to Pestek's crime—an alibi they could produce for their superiors. One day, in September, Schwarzhuber suddenly brought my interrogation to an end and sentenced me to a penal company for life. There I had to work very hard in a penal squad *(Grabenbau)* digging trenches.

"On October 26, 1944, however, my friends helped smuggle me in a prisoners' transport to a working camp in Bavaria, where I was liberated in spring 1945 by the American soldiers. My twisted fingers and the other marks of ill treatment on my body will remain with me until death as a visible reminder of the extermination camp Auschwitz-Birkenau."

Chapter 21

To the Partisans in Slovakia

LEDERER DID NOT STAY in Prague long. He went to Bohusovice. He weighed the situation and came to the conclusion that the Theresienstadt ghetto was the safest hiding place of all. He lived in the loft of the fire house, and Holzer and Petschauer brought him his food. He became the nucleus of a dedicated resistance movement. His optimism, dauntlessness, and audacity encouraged his followers. Secret collections of money for arms purchases were organized in the camp. The women surrendered their wedding rings and jewels. Connections with other resistance groups in the country were good.

Lederer's message to the International Red Cross in Switzerland apparently reached its destination. (His report was not the only one. It had been confirmed and supplemented by a report of two other Auschwitz prisoners, Alfred Wetzler and Rudolf Vrba, who succeeded in escaping from Birkenau to Slovakia five days after Lederer.) The International Red Cross in Geneva wrote to the Foreign Ministry in Berlin through the mediation of the Swiss government and asked for an explanation. The Nazis once again declared it to be a fabrication and merely hostile propaganda. But the Red Cross was not satisfied. They wanted an international delegation to see the concentration camps for themselves.

The Nazi foreign minister took the matter very seriously. He asked the RSHA in Berlin to help supply proof for the German embassy so they could deny these *Greulnachrichten* (scare mongers' propaganda).

The Allied press and the Soviet and British broadcasting stations brought out detailed accounts of what was happening in the concentration camps and disclosed the Heydebreck play used at Auschwitz. This induced both SS Reichsfuehrer Himmler and the main coordinator of the "final solution," Adolf Eichmann, to be more careful.

The intended mass liquidation of the December transport from Theresienstadt was not carried out. When the six-month quarantine period expired, Schwarzhuber came to the family camp with Dr. Mengele and Dr. Lucas. This time they recruited the prisoners for work. They chose more than a thousand healthy men and sent them to perish during the building of underground aircraft factories near the concentration camp Schwarzheide. Two thousand healthy childless women were sent to the Stutthof concentration camp to do harvesting and to dig antitank trenches. Another thousand women were sent to clear away unexploded bombs and bombed-out houses near Hamburg. René Karen and her mother were among them. The prisoners were ordered to write to their friends from these places. The remaining prisoners in the family camp—the women with children and those considered unfit to work—died on July 10 and 12, 1944 in the gas chambers just as those who preceded them in March.

In June 1944, Adolf Eichmann came to Theresienstadt with Deputy Foreign Minister von Thadden and Protectorate Minister K. H. Frank. He examined the ghetto to see whether it was fit to welcome the international commission. Theresienstadt had changed entirely. Things had greatly improved during the last months. Houses and streets had been renovated. The deportations to the east had stopped. Shops were full of goods. The bank of Theresienstadt issued new bank notes. Previously confiscated food parcels from the Red Cross were now delivered. The SS commander of the Theresienstadt ghetto exchanged his uniform for a business suit in an attempt to show that he was merely head of a civilian administration. Care for the sick and for the children improved, too. Theater performances, concerts, and lectures were organized. Everybody looked forward to the Red Cross visit. They believed that it would herald their salvation. The broadcasts from abroad that they listened to, along with the fantasies they nurtured, strengthened the prisoners' hopes that the end of the war was at hand.

The visit was a great success for the Nazis. They could not have wished for a better report than that given by one of the delegates of the International Red Cross, Dr. M. Rossels:* " . . . This Jewish town is most remarkable. The Jewish population speaks many different languages and have come from different surroundings, various conditions, and a variety of social backgrounds. It was necessary to create a spirit of unity. That was very difficult. The ghetto of Theresienstadt is a 'Communist' community. Its 'Stalin' is a man of great merit: his name is Dr. Epstein . . . "

Berlin decided to exploit this success by shooting a film about life in Theresienstadt. The aim of the film was to convince the moviegoers that all the news about the extermination of Jews was pure fabrication. One of the prisoners, Kurt Geron, wrote the script, in accordance with the directions he received from Hans Guenther, the commander of the Prague Emigration Center. The filming was done by Prague film producers and cameramen. Some prisoners assisted, and the whole team was supervised by Gestapo men disguised as film assistants.

The film began with a historical account of how the fortress of Theresienstadt had been built under Emperor Joseph II and how the town had grown and developed. Then followed some arranged scenes depicting the arrival of transports to the "spa" of Theresienstadt; the part about the life of the population ended with a scene showing a train bringing food supplies to the ghetto and taking away the products of the Theresienstadt prisoners.

The main part of the film was made up of cleverly distorted scenes of the ghetto inhabitants' rich and joyful life: harvesting in the valley of Bohusovice, pretty young women from Theresienstadt cultivating tomato crops, the working of the central laundry, and the training of the fire brigade. In the streets of Theresienstadt the camera met former ministers, generals, and other important dignitaries from Germany, Austria, France, and Czechoslovakia, whose incarceration in the ghetto was due to the racial laws. They were seen again on the terrace of the "club house" during their afternoon "siesta." Well-known, learned European men could be seen listening to a lecture given by Dr. Emil Utitz, a professor at Prague University. There were many shots of the library.

The life of the children in Theresienstadt was filmed in a most convincing manner. For this purpose, great sums of money were spent to decorate a big house formerly occupied by an SS officer. The house was to be filmed as the Children's Home. The children were shown coming from the marketplace with two young governesses in white cloaks. The

*H. G. Adler, *Verheimlichte Warheit* (Tubingen: J. C. B. Mohr Verlag, 1958), pp. 354 ff.

procession passed along the bank and the shops, with their nicely arranged windows, and came to a playground bordered with trees and palms in big flowerpots. The children frolicked about, played in the sand, sat on rocking horses, rode on tricycles, climbed on merry-go-rounds and slides. Then they took a rest on deck chairs or camp beds under the trees of the "Children's Home" garden. Nurses came and brought slices of bread and butter and tomatoes on trays. But the children rushed toward them and ate everything up before there was time for the cameramen to shoot. They had to wait for another batch of bread and butter to be prepared for the filming.

A swimming pool was built solely for the film. The running and working of the bank and of the post office, the dancing in the coffeehouse, the performance of *Hoffmann's Tales* and of a children's opera were staged in the same manner. Addresses and speeches were made at a special festive meeting of the ghetto self-government. Family life was depicted in a luxurious flat of one of the prominent prisoners rather than in the overcrowded dwellings and lofts crammed with bunks. Three thousand spectators were commanded to watch a soccer match between two nonexistent teams. Some parts of Theresienstadt looked like Hollywood. It was proposed that the International Red Cross also visit the Jewish labor camp at Birkenau. But the positive impression left by the Theresienstadt ghetto "satisfied all their expectations," and rendered a visit to Arbeitslager Birkenau by the International Red Cross superfluous.*

The cultural life of Theresienstadt grew enormously. Food parcels prevented the usual hunger. The transports to the east were nearly forgotten. The measures suggested by the resistance group were now meaningless. The liquidation of the ghetto did not seem imminent. Enthusiasm waned, the spirit of rebellion subsided. A feeling of security grew stronger and stronger. Even in Holzer's flat, the following statement could be heard: "The Germans are done for. The war is going to end soon, and it would be suicide to rebel. It's no use to prepare a massacre."

The rabbi rarely came to see the Holzers. Soon after the visit of the international commission, he had come to give them a warning. A dangerous partisan scare monger was said to be hiding in the ghetto; this has been discussed at a secret meeting of the Elder's Council. The SS commander promised freedom and a reward for his disclosure.

Lederer felt that it was no longer safe for him to stay in the ghetto. It

---

* Otto Dov Kulka, "Ghetto in an Annihilation Camp," published in *The Nazi Concentration Camps* (Jerusalem: Yad Vashem, 1984), pp. 315–30.

became difficult and dangerous to conceal him. He returned to his hiding place in the Zbraslav cabin.

The resistance movement around Zbraslav was getting stronger as the front grew nearer. Mican and Pokorny recruited more members for their group. One of them was Adolf Kopriva, caretaker of the villa near Lederer's cabin where he went to stay on the weekends.

One day, at the end of July, Lederer appeared at the inn. Mican was surprised to see him. He called the committee members. They listened to Lederer's account of the unsuccessful expedition to Auschwitz and conditions in Theresienstadt.

"Good thing you have come," said Mican. "You won't be bored here."

Then they set up a plan for how to best use Lederer's cover as an SS officer for sabotage and resistance activities.

"In the Roederstein factory here in Zbraslav," said Pokorny, "spare parts for the Luftwaffe are being made day and night. It would be good if you could see to it that they are made a little bit slower."

Pesek the baker said, "The Prague firm SS Baustandarte have a lot of building sites along the route from Prague to Stechovice. They are full of iron, wood, and cement. You could have a look at what could be done there. Plenty of our people are working at the building sites."

"I accept both commissions," Lederer said, "but I'll need somebody to show me the building in question."

"You know Adolf Kopriva," said Mican. "He's working as a driver for the SS Baustandarte."

While the Nazis were searching in vain for the escaped prisoner from Birkenau, Lederer, as SS Obersturmfuehrer Welker, was "supervising" the building sites in a black Steyer limousine driven by Kopriva.

The Germans in Zbraslav had stopped isolating themselves. They announced that it was necessary to pull down the barriers between nations. They even asked the innkeeper to remove the wooden wall of the casino. Meanwhile, the resistance group was growing stronger, and Lederer was feeling more secure.

One evening in August, however, he was reminded that he was still a fugitive. An SS squad burst into the inn. Two SS officers with tommy guns stood at the door, guarding the entrance. The SS Scharfuehrer first paid homage to the Fuehrer and then exclaimed, "Everyone take out your papers! Nobody is allowed to leave the room!"

The SS, fully armed, aimed their machine guns at the frightened patrons. At the same time another officer began checking papers at the nearest table. Mican grew visibly pale: he was thinking of the partisans sitting in his inn, the sabotage material in the attic, the arms in the cellar, and his wife and children sleeping upstairs in the bedroom. Not one of the paralyzed patrons could think of anything to prevent the inevitable disaster.

Only one of them was not flustered and kept his cool. He was not afraid. Dressed in an SS officer's uniform, he rose from his chair and approached the commander of the squad. He saluted, raising his right hand, and said, "I'd like to talk to you privately, Scharfuehrer!"

All eyes were turned in their direction as they left the room. Lederer reproved the Scharfuehrer. Tersely, in his faultless Berlin-accented German, he asked whether the Scharfueher realized that his behavior was disturbing, in a most impertinent way, the friendly relationship that had been established between the Czech and German populations, which was most cordial in this region and extremely important for the war effort as well. He, Lederer, would not like to see the good relations disturbed in any way. He was responsible for an important section of buildings of the SS Baustandarte, and the Scharfuehrer's intervention might be a negative influence on the morale of the people.

"If you don't have a special order, Scharfuehrer," said Lederer, "I suggest you stop causing trouble."

Lederer, holding Welker's identity card in his hand, said, "By the way, I would not like to bring up this incident tomorrow at a meeting in the Reichsprotektor's office."

The Scharfuehrer did not even look at Lederer's identity card. He clicked his heels, saluted, went back to the saloon, and said loudly, "We have finished here! Withdraw!"

He saluted again, raising his hand, and left the inn with his men.

Lederer's desperate deed saved the resistance group in Zbraslav for the moment. Nevertheless, it was likely that the night's events would be reported and that the Gestapo would immediately start looking for Welker, realizing that he was an imposter. Mican called a meeting, and they discussed what should be done. The situation was dangerous. Pesck suggested, "Siegfried must disappear from Bohemia. The best thing for him to do is to try to join the partisans in Slovakia."

They all agreed.

Mican said to Lederer, "You will go through Ceska Trebova and Olomouc to Moravia. In the district of Vsetin, near the village of Hovezi, you will find an isolated house in the woods. It belongs to Martin Simcik, the gamekeeper. You will tell him the password and who has sent you, and he will lead you safely over the border to Slovakia."

Lederer wasted no time. He went to his cabin, changed into civilian clothes, and left at midnight from Prague to Hranice by express train.

From there he took a local train to Vsetin, where he learned that the German frontier guards checked the papers of all passengers in the train going to Hovezi. He therefore decided to go on foot, and reached Simcik's house after a three-hour walk. He gave the password (*Kychova*) and was invited to come in.

Martin Simcik was a broad-shouldered man, a typical highlander from the Valachia Mountains. He did not speak much, but offered Lederer a can of milk and a piece of sheep cheese, took his walking stick, and off they went through the valley of Kychova to the mountains of Javorniky. In two hours they reached a mountain chalet (*Kohutka*) that was close to the frontier between Moravia and Slovakia. Simcik went first to reconnoiter. The chalet was occupied by German frontier guards (*Greko*). They had to wait for the change of guards.

Lederer and Simcik climbed up to an observation tower placed high up among two fir trees from which hunters observed game. The *Greko* sentries could be seen from there. The two men lay in wait until the guards changed shifts. Then they ran quickly to Slovak ground. Simcik introduced Lederer to a Slovak partisan named Belak and returned home.

Belak, too, lived in an isolated house in the woods. In the evening he took Lederer to the village. There Lederer told the villagers all about himself and his adventures. They liked him. The village was the center of volunteers who trained to fight against the Nazis and the Slovak Hlinka Guard.

Lederer became a member of a partisan group. Their job was to distract the *Greko* while a large group of partisans crossed the frontier.

One day, Lederer was wounded in a skirmish. A bullet penetrated his foot and lodged above the ankle. He crawled to a fallen fir tree and lay under its thick green brushwood. He called for help, but to no avail. He dragged himself and hobbled along from one tree to another, but soon he lost his way. Then at last he saw the chalet of *Kohutka*. He was on the path that he had taken with Simcik.

Lederer's ankle did not hurt as much anymore, but his whole foot was swollen. He could not pull off his boot. For six hours Lederer limped along the road through the Kychova valley to the isolated cottage of Simcik the gamekeeper and fell exhausted in front of the door to the cowshed. There Simcik's wife found him when she went to feed the cattle in the evening. The gamekeeper carried Lederer's limp body upstairs to the loft and laid him on some straw. He loosened Lederer's clothes and checked his pulse. His heartbeat seemed very faint. Then Simcik pried Lederer's mouth open and poured a large draught of brandy down his throat. Slowly the injured man began to show signs of life. When he came to, Lederer showed Simcik his gun wound and asked him to take the boot off his swollen foot. Simcik cut the boot open with a sharp knife, then removed it carefully to examine the wound by gaslight. The bullet was lodged deep inside, and the wound was inflamed; yet it was out of the question to call a doctor or take him to a hospital. So Simcik bound Lederer's arms and hands, knelt down, and performed the operation himself. He cut the wound open and pried out the bullet, using a knife heated in the fire as a scalpel. Brandy served as the sole disinfectant and narcotic. After bandaging the wound, Simcik removed a partition in the wooden wall of the double roof and hid Lederer in the narrow passageway inside. He put him on a straw mattress and covered him with a quilt. Lederer was running a high fever and there was a danger of infection.

In his delirium, Lederer had hallucinations of grisly scenes from Auschwitz, and visions of his life flashed before him as in a film. He asked himself who was the more unfortunate: the Birkenau prisoners and victims, or the eternally outcast Jew? What was the good of his escape? Whom had he helped? Whose life could he save? How many of his friends had he endangered? In his imagination, he saw Pestek firing from the train window and quarreling with SS officers. Had he fallen in the fight, or had they taken him alive? He suffered as he imagined Pestek being tortured during the Gestapo interrogation. Did Pestek betray those who had given them refuge? And what was the fate of the family camp? Did they revolt in June when Schwarzhuber and Mengele began to prepare the second liquidation of the December transport? What happened to René? Was Lederer's partisan group successful in the Slovak uprising? Did his friends in Plzen evade the Gestapo? Lederer reproached himself for having endangered Vesely's family in Travcice for nothing. In the ghetto he had failed utterly: those on the verge of annihilation would not believe him, grasping at Nazi lies like drowning men. He had not succeeded in the ghetto, but what about the effect of his message on the International Red Cross in Switzerland? Those who read his report did not live behind fortress walls and electrified barbed wire fences. What were they doing to stop the mass murders in Auschwitz?

Lederer choked at his own powerlessness and damned the indifference of all those in the free world with the power to act. He tormented himself all night with the question of how to find influential people and how to get them to act on the atrocities of Auschwitz.

In the midst of Lederer's torments, Simcik came to visit him in his hiding place. Perched on the edge of his straw mattress, he reported with emotion, "Just now the BBC broadcast from London exactly what you told me about Auschwitz. The Allies have warned the Nazis to stop the deportations and gassings. They declared that everyone involved in murdering defenseless civilians would be tried and severely punished after the war."

Lederer strained to hear, devouring every word. "And so . . . perhaps . . . all our efforts were not in vain," he mumbled, as though to himself. And for the first time in a long while, he fell into a sound sleep.

Thanks to Mrs. Simcik's devoted care, the crisis passed, and Lederer's wound slowly healed at the solitary cottage in the woods. After his recovery, Lederer returned to Zbraslav to look for his friends from Weidman's group. With some of them Lederer had served in a partisan unit operating in the Brdy forest, fighting the Germans there until defeating them.

In May 1945, after some German POWs had been questioned, Lederer learned of the whereabouts of the children abducted from Lidice, whose murdered fathers he had buried in a mass grave two years earlier. Lederer checked the list and found the name Eva Kubikova, a relative of the Czerniks from Plzen, who had helped him and Pestek during their escape. On Lederer's initiative, a small volunteer group was formed and went immediately to Germany to search for the girl. They drove through the ruins of the defeated country, looking for Czech children who had been placed with Nazi families for "reeducation." Among them six-year-old Eva Kubikova was found. In the meantime, Eva's mother had been liberated from Ravensbrueck, and at the first memorial service in Lidice, in June 1945, Lederer handed little Eva over to her happy mother.

Lederer was honored and decorated for his bravery. He married and returned to his prewar profession, as a leading expert in a textile firm in Prague. He also tried to gain some political influence for Weidman's resistance group and was generally active in politics on behalf of his democratic party. After the Prague Communist coup in February 1948, the national democratic Weidman group was disbanded and its members persecuted. In the following years, during the Slansky trial (1951–53), strong anti-Semitic propaganda launched by the Communist party caused Lederer to be fired from his job. He was scarcely able to find a modest position as a salesman in a textile company. Frustrated and exhausted by the vain fight for his and his friends' rehabilitation, he retired and withdrew from all public activities and led a modest life with his wife and son in a small villa in the Prague suburb of Sporilov.

Lederer died at age sixty-eight on April 5, 1972, exactly twenty-eight years after his dramatic escape from Auschwitz. His body was cremated at a small service attended by his family and a few friends in Prague. Not a single notice appeared in the Czech media.

Postscript

IN 1966, when the Czech version of this book first appeared, most of the people in the story were still alive. The following information is for those readers interested in the fate of some of the people in this true story.

René Karen was interrogated by the Auschwitz Gestapo after Pestek's arrest, but was not punished. In the course of the second liquidation of the family camp, René and her mother, along with a thousand women from that camp, were deported from Birkenau to work in a concentration camp near Hamburg. Both returned to Prague after the liberation, where René married an American officer in 1946 and moved to the United States with her mother.

Most of those who helped the fugitives in Bohemia were also still living in 1966: Mr. and Mrs. Cernik; Gitta Skala, whose real name was Brigitta Steiner (married name Kroftova); and Eduard Kotora, one of the founders of the Weidman group. Of the others, Pepik Pokorny, Antonin Pesek, and Adolf Kopriva were living in Zbraslav. Chief Constable Jicha and the innkeeper Mican both died in 1961. The cabin that served as a hiding place for the escapees was rebuilt, and its owner, Ada Kroupa, lives in Prague. Also living in Prague are the following: engineer Leo Holzer (chief of the fire brigade at Theresienstadt ghetto); and Dr. Alfred Milek and the pharmacist Ludvik Sand, from the family camp. Lederer's barracks deputy Miroslav Zeimer, and the informer from *Sonderkommando,* Filip Mueller, live in West Germany.

Of the Birkenau criminals, SS Commander Johann Schwarzhuber and Rapportfuehrers Buntrock and Krupanek were sentenced to death and executed. The Zyklon murderer, Josef Klehr, was sentenced to life imprisonment. SS physician Bernhard Lucas was tried in Frankfurt and sentenced to four years' imprisonment. His colleague, SS Dr. Josef Mengele, has never been found, but according to recent news reports Mengele died by drowning on February 7, 1979 in Brazil. He had lived under the name Wolfgang Gerhard, and was buried in São Paulo. On June 6, 1985 the grave was opened, the body exhumed, and the skull and bones allegedly verified by forensic experts as the remains of Mengele.

APPENDIX

About the Author

ERICH KULKA was born 18 February 1911 in Vestin, Moravia (Czechoslovakia) to parents who were very active members of the Jewish community. After completing high school and technical studies, Kulka worked in the lumber industry, becoming the manager of a saw mill by 1937.

In June 1939 Kulka was arrested by the Gestapo for anti-Nazi activities. He was deported to a succession of concentration camps —Dachau, Hamburg-Neuengamme, arriving finally at Auschwitz-Birkenau in October 1942. He obtained a job as a locksmith in the prisoner-maintenance work squad, which enabled him to observe the workings and, ultimately, the final dismantling of the detention and extermination complex at Auschwitz-Birkenau.

In January 1945, in the course of the evacuation chaos of camp prisoners, Kulka and his son Otto succeeded in escaping. Kulka's wife, Elly, had earlier been moved to the Stutthof camp where she died.

After the war, Kulka testified against the SS war criminals in numerous international trials. He was decorated by the Czech Ministry of Defense for his resistance activities and was elected Chairman of

Antifascist Fighters. He also co-authored (with Ota Kraus) his first book *The Death Factory—Document on Auschwitz*, which has been published in eight languages.

In 1947 Kulka married his sister-in-law Olga, whose first husband died in the Neuengamme camp. Wishing to emigrate to Israel to join his son, Otto, and his brother, Kulka and his wife were repeatedly denied permission by the Czechoslovakian authorities. In 1951, during the communist antisemitic campaign, Kulka was fired from his job as department manager in a state wood products enterprise in Prague.

Faced with few prospects of employment in such a strongly antisemitic atmosphere, Kulka resumed his activities as a researcher and historian of anti-Nazi resistance. He published numerous books and articles in Czechoslovakia and abroad.

The "Prague Spring" of 1968 forced Kulka to move to Vienna, which he did with the help of his friend Simon Wiesenthal. By the end of 1968, Kulka and his entire family were able to leave Austria and settle in Israel.

In Jerusalem, Kulka is presently associated with the Yad Vashem Museum and the Institute for Contemporary Jewry, and he is Honorary Chairman of the Public Committee of Survivors of Auschwitz. Through his writing and research activities, Kulka continues his effort to protect and promote the truth of his experience and of our history.

Birkenau
20 June 1944

My Dearest!—

On the last night of my life I bid you farewell. Our happiness has been short-lived, but wonderful. I recall our love from its beautiful beginning until its cruel end. You have been the greatest happiness of my life, and I would gladly give my life to save yours. And our little innocent Otik, why should his short life be ended by such a cruel, brutal hand!

As the end draws near, I remember our dear one. If you meet them again, tell them I kiss them a thousand times, my beloved sister, my brother and Olinka, Max and Lydia, and especially Danecek and Lianka. I wish them a happier life than ours has been. May they fight courageously for our freedom and revenge the innocent blood of their dear ones.

Thank you, my darling, with all my heart for the devotion, love and joy you have given me. Always remain what you are—a courageous, unbreakable hero. I shall think of you and pray for your safety until my last breath. Give my last thoughts and greetings to all your comrades.

Farewell, beloved! We kiss you for the last time, your Elly and your little Oticek! Goodbye.

Note: Kulka received this letter from his wife, Elly, while he was in Birkenau camp B-II-d. He later sent it illegally, in August 1944 (along with the letter that follows), to his sister-in-law Olga (later, his wife) who was in hiding in Moravia. The letters were smuggled out of Birkenau by Kulka's non-Jewish countryman Thomas Marak, who worked in the Birkenau camp area as a building expert for a construction firm.

Birkenau
2 August 1944

Dear Oli!—

I am using perhaps the last opportunity to brief you about our fate. Palma, Boris and our grandmother have perished by violent death in the course of the extermination of the September 1943 transport from Theresienstadt Ghetto. It was a miracle when I succeeded in rescuing Elly and Otik. Also, I managed to save them from the second liquidation in June 1944, which was unexpectedly more modest (the younger, childless women were selected for work). Elly was deported to another concentration camp in Stutthof, near Danzig, and Otik is with me here. Ernst is alive and he is bearing very hard the tragic loss of his dearest. Our situation here is extremely critical and we can survive only by a miracle. According to the prevailing pattern, it is especially certain that they will exterminate us, the direct witnesses of this horrible crime. I am enclosing Elly's farewell letter, which she sent me a day before the expected liquidation. In the very last moment she was rescued and is alive as mentioned above. The front is coming nearer and we, the defenseless, are anxious what will happen to us. In any case I am enclosing my last will, so that my property should be inherited by your children. Greetings and kisses to all of you.

Erich and Otik

Note: Thomas Marak smuggled this letter out of Birkenau when he was granted permission by the SS to visit his family in Nedakonice, Moravia. He was closely watched by the Gestapo. Only after he returned to Auschwitz-Birkenau did his wife travel to Novy Hrozenkov and deliver the letter to Olga. In a similar way, Kulka and others smuggled out of the camp the exact lay-out of the Nazi extermination installation.

Thomas Marak's identity card, issued by the SS, which permitted him to enter the Auschwitz area.